43RD BIENNIAL EXHIBITION OF CONTEMPORARY AMERICAN PAINTING

ORGANIZED BY

Terrie Sultan

WITH CONTRIBUTIONS BY

Maia Damianovic

Judith Russi Kirshner

Klaus Ottmann

David Pagel

Maria Porges

Marla Price

Gary Sangster

Lowery Stokes Sims

Alisa Tager

EDITED BY

Christopher C. French

43RD BIENNIAL EXHIBITION OF CONTEMPORARY AMERICAN

PAINTING

THE CORCORAN GALLERY OF ART

HUNG LIU
JIM LUTES
KERRY JAMES MARSHALL
MELISSA MILLER
MANUEL OCAMPO
DEBORAH OROPALLO
ELENA SISTO
NANCY SPERO

IDA APPLEBROOG
KEN APTEKAR
DOTTY ATTIE
LUIS CRUZ AZACETA
DONALD BAECHLER
BEATTIE & DAVIDSON
PHYLLIS BRAMSON
MICHAEL BYRON
CAROLE CAROOMPAS
ROBERT COLESCOTT
KIM DINGLE
INGA FRICK
CHARLES GARABEDIAN
LEON GOLUB
CATHERINE HOWE
DAVID HUMPHREY

This book has been published in conjunction with
the *43rd Biennial Exhibition of Contemporary
American Painting*, organized by The Corcoran
Gallery of Art, and serves as catalogue for the exhibition.

The Corcoran Gallery of Art
Washington, D.C.
October 30, 1993–January 2, 1994

Both the exhibition and book have been made
possible in part by the Anna E. Clark Fund, The
Friends of the Corcoran, and by Deane and
Paul Shatz.

Additional support for the catalogue has been
generously provided by the Elizabeth Firestone
Graham Foundation.

In 1927 Anna E. Clark, the widow of Senator
William A. Clark, established a fund for the per-
petuation of the Biennial.

The Corcoran Gallery of Art
17th Street & New York Avenue, N.W.
Washington, D.C. 20006

Editor/publication manager:
Christopher C. French
Exhibition coordinator: Shannon Morse
Catalogue design: Cynthia Hotvedt

Library of Congress Catalog
Card Number 93-79576
ISBN: 0-88675-040-7

C O N T E N T S

LENDERS TO THE EXHIBITION

Harry W. and Mary Margaret Anderson

ARA Services

Josh Baer Gallery, New York

The Bailey Collection

The Barrett Collection

Claudio and Paola Bordignon

Rena Bransten Gallery, San Francisco

Brody's Gallery, Washington, D.C.

Edie and James Cloonan

Jeffrey A. Dash

Eric and Barbara Dobkin

Germans Van Eck Gallery, New York

Ronald Feldman Fine Arts, New York

Frumkin/Adams Gallery, New York

Galerie Philippe Gravier, Paris

Gallery Paule Anglim, San Francisco

Fred Hoffman Fine Art, Los Angeles

Susan and Michael Hort

Jones Troyer Fitzpatrick Gallery,
Washington, D.C.

Paul Kasmin Gallery, New York

Phyllis Kind Gallery, New York and
Chicago

Klinger - Gal Collection

Koplin Gallery, Los Angeles

L.A. Louver, Inc., Venice, California

Anne MacDonald

McKee Gallery, New York

P.P.O.W., New York

Tom Patchett

Jay Pidto and Lynne Baer

Jean Pigozzi

Alan P. Power

The Principal Financial Group

Madeline Murphy Rabb

Arthur G. Rosen

Rubell Family Collections, New York

Mr. and Mrs. Robert Sager

Frances Scher

Jack Shainman Gallery, New York

Charles Sims

Sue Spaid Fine Art, Los Angeles

Steinbaum Krauss Gallery, New York

Texas Gallery, Houston

Edward Thorp Gallery, New York

Alan Wanzenberg

Bob and Heather Westendarp

Sperone Westwater Gallery, New York

43RD BIENNIAL EXHIBITION OF CONTEMPORARY AMERICAN PAINTING

The Corcoran Biennial, now in its 86th year, is one of our nation's oldest exhibitions series. By its exclusive focus limited to those paintings produced in America during the preceding two years, the exhi-

F O R E W O R D

bition establishes a contemporary flavor on a national scale. This is of direct consequence not only to our nation's capital city and its broad constituencies but also to the many students in our own School of Art. Other bi-annual surveys—Venice, Sao Paulo, the Carnegie, or the Whitney, for example—present a variety of media, frequently ranging far afield with intentionally contrary and mixed agendas. By comparison, the Corcoran's Biennial is shaped to provide points of reconciliation and curatorial clarity concerning the fundamentals of artistic quality and achievement found in the painted arts.

The best Biennials are about discovery, framed by a confident belief in the importance of our recurring critical expertise. The Corcoran's 1991 Biennial was a close inspection of abstract painting. Organized by Terrie Sultan, curator of contemporary art, that challenging exhibition presented thirteen artists whose various individual styles pushed at the boundaries of gestural and formal abstraction.

This year, as counterpoint, Ms. Sultan embarked on an ambitious mission to tackle the various natures of figuration. In so doing, the current Biennial is not only the obverse of our last Biennial, it diverges from a number of our previous Biennials of the 1960s and 1970s, which were dominated by stylized abstraction.

This 43rd Corcoran Biennial draws attention to the complicated systems of overt and covert images and figures used to communicate and effect our lives. The twenty-five artists chosen comprise a vast exhibition extending through all the Corcoran's special display galleries. These artists employ depictions of the figure not as a still-life studio prop, but as a form freighted with provocative personal and social meaning. However, final authority has been given to those paintings that function best as works of art, rather than platforms of propaganda. This marriage of form and content would seem to be an important, timely, contribution to the ongoing discussion of the role of art and society.

To demonstrate the importance and hardy pervasiveness of this figural attitude during the past three decades, we have included mature artists as well as mid-career and younger artists. Though different in many respects, the works chosen for this exhibition have curious and compelling points where they interlock, building one upon the other to achieve a complex dialogue of form and message about our shared condition.

The talented artists included here offer a wide palette of interpretation and engagement. I want to recognize them for their profound qualities of invention and Ms. Sultan for her skill, energy, and vision in bringing this exhibition to fruition.

JACK COWART
Deputy Director,
Chief Curator

11

The idea to focus on figurative representation as the central theme for the 43rd Biennial Exhibition of Contemporary American Painting developed out of conversations with artists I visited over the

PREFACE AND ACKNOWLEDGEMENTS

course of a two year research period. While the practice of painting in America remains vibrantly and profoundly varied, this exhibition is intended to demonstrate what I feel is one of the most important and compelling aspects of the full panoply of painterly expression.

A project of the scope and complexity of this exhibition and the catalogue that accompanies it could not have been realized without the enthusiasm of a number of individuals, all of whom gave unceasingly of their time and energy. I would like to express my appreciation to Maia Damianovic, Judith Russi Kirshner, Klaus Ottmann, David Pagel, Maria Porges, Marla Price, Gary Sangster, Lowery Stokes Sims, and Alisa Tager for their concise and insightful essays, which contribute a depth of understanding to the work of the participating artists. As overall editor of the catalogue, Christopher French worked diligently to control the voluminous details, providing a voice of reason through careful and sensitive editing for me and nine highly individual writers; Joanna Eckman ably assisted in the editing of my essay. Cynthia Hotvedt achieved a cohesive and elegant catalogue design.

The members of the Corcoran staff have significantly contributed to the accomplishment of this project. David C. Levy, president and director, and Jack Cowart, deputy director and chief curator both provided astute advice and moral support that sustained my progress. Victoria Larson supplied expertise on administration and budget matters; Marisa Keller assisted with

research and Johanna Karelis with proofreading. Cindy Rom and Julie Solz managed the complex arrangements for shipping from private collections, museums, and galleries in the United States and abroad. Clyde Paton and Greg Angelone ably handled the installation, and Cedric Miller masterly solved a number of intricate lighting problems. I would especially like to thank Shannon Morse for her capable assistance in coordinating countless details of research, correspondence, loan agreements, and photographic attributions, and for her dedication and attention in producing the artists' biographies and bibliographies.

My thanks also to the private collectors who generously agreed to share their works with the public for this exhibition, and to the galleries and their staffs for their help in securing loans. Their enthusiastic participation is much appreciated.

Funds for the 43rd Biennial Exhibition of Contemporary American Painting were provided by the Anna E. Clark Fund, The Friends of the Corcoran, and by Deane and Paul Shatz. The Elizabeth Firestone Graham Foundation generously supported the publication of the exhibition catalogue. We are very grateful for their dedication and commitment to the project.

Finally, I would like to express my heartfelt thanks to the participating artists. They shared their time, energy, and ideas with me, making this project a true partnership. It has been my privilege to work with them.

TERRIE SULTAN
Curator of
Contemporary Art

13

> **Written on the body is a secret code only visible in certain lights; the accumulations of a lifetime gather there.**
> **—Jeanette Winterson**[1]

THE THEMES THAT REFLECT US

Since the advent of Abstract Expressionism, artists, especially painters, who have focused on the figure have found themselves strangely at odds with prevailing stylistic and conceptual hierarchies, which have concentrated on abstraction, appropriation from popular media sources, or sculptural installations incorporating the viewer as the central, activating character. In the past several years, however, a number of artists have begun to gain prominence for their emphasis on figurative modes of representation. Almost all recent discussion of this issue has centered on sculptural idioms, but as this Biennial Exhibition of Contemporary American Painting demonstrates, figuration remains an essential aspect of the current aesthetic of painting as well. For the twenty-three artists and one collaborative team brought together here, the body is the juncture at which form and content collide.

The careers of the painters included in this exhibition, spanning some forty years, represent a continuum across generations. Leon Golub, Nancy Spero, Robert Colescott, Charles Garabedian, and Ida Applebroog gained their first successes in the 1950s and early 1960s. For them, representational imagery, often turned to after initial forays into abstraction, provides a fulcrum for meditations on a wide variety of social and political issues. A second generation, including artists such as Dotty Attie, Luis Cruz Azaceta, Phyllis Bramson, Carole Caroompas, and Hung Liu first exhibited in the 1970s and early 1980s. Their art treats the body in a more personal way, invoking both mythology and autobiography. The influences of these two approaches can be seen in the work of younger artists such as Ken Aptekar, Donald Baechler, Drew Beattie & Daniel Davidson, Michael Byron, Kim Dingle, Inga Frick, Catherine Howe, David Humphrey, Jim Lutes, Kerry James Marshall, Melissa Miller, Manuel Ocampo, Deborah Oropallo, and Elena Sisto. While seeking to push the boundaries of their medium in new directions, these artists continue to embrace the painted figure as the ultimate metaphor for the human condition.

The guise of two-dimensionality, which requires that we approach a painting frontally and directly, produces a set of responses different from that elicited by sculpture, with its often sensual tactility and multiple perspectives; the slow, cognitive read painting offers is at variance with sculpture's more visceral gestalt. The artists represented here have all developed highly personalized reactions to the challenge of representation enunciated through the medium of painting, and in their work words often serve as a connective bridge between form and content. Language provides narrative markers in the paintings of Attie, Aptekar, and Oropallo, and is used by Colescott, Golub, and Ocampo to make biting provocations or humorous critiques. For others, the figure-ground interaction alone acts as the mapping device that charts the narrative surface of the human body. Looking, for each of these artists, is never

TERRIE SULTAN

15

a purely visual process, and for many, the inter-relationship of language and figurative images reinforces our desire to comprehensively "read" their pictures.

The diverse approaches to painting in this exhibition include the process-oriented, layer-and-scrape attack of Leon Golub; the heightened attention to traditional materials and techniques in the work of Ida Applebroog, Kim Dingle, Charles Garabedian, Jim Lutes, Kerry James Marshall, Melissa Miller, Deborah Oropallo, and Elena Sisto; the photographic sources and collage techniques used by Luis Cruz Azaceta, Donald Baechler, Phyllis Bramson, Michael Byron, Carole Caroompas, Inga Frick, David Humphrey, Hung Liu, and Nancy Spero; the collaborative teamwork of Drew Beattie & Daniel Davidson; and the acknowledgment of historical styles in the work of Dotty Attie, Ken Aptekar, Robert Colescott, Catherine Howe, and Manuel Ocampo. From these cross-cutting stylistic approaches, two central themes emerge. On the one hand, the human form functions as a metaphoric vehicle, conveying political or social content through pictorial tableaux or juxtapositions of image and text. On the other hand, the figure represents inner states of being, often theatrically expanding or even reinventing accepted definitions of self. In both cases, these artists have chosen figurative models because they best express the central dilemma of present-day life: the changing nature of the roles and responsibilities available to the individual in society, and the psychic or social cost of attaining and maintaining individuality.

* * *

Figuration, by its nature, relies upon the extrinsic traces of the culture that produces it. American artists working in the figurative style have a certain assertiveness, frankness, openness—language that Americans flatter themselves with.
—Leon Golub[2]

When addressing the figure, artists working today must recognize the lengthy history of representation in painting and decide whether to challenge this history, to incorporate its perspectives through appropriation, or to deliberately subvert it. The influence of the tradition of social commentary in Western painting, which can be traced to the Classical and Romantic movements of the eighteenth and nineteenth centuries, can be seen in the social or political gestures that inform the art of Ken Aptekar, Ida Applebroog, Dotty Attie, Luis Cruz Azaceta, Carole Caroompas, Robert Colescott, Kim Dingle, Charles Garabedian, Leon Golub, Catherine Howe, Hung Liu, Kerry James Marshall, Manuel Ocampo, and Nancy Spero. While acknowledging the value of past traditions, these artists consciously depart from the historicized narratives of Francisco Goya, Jacques-Louis David, Théodore Géricault, Gustave Courbet, and Pablo Picasso, which, like the work of a philosophical reporter, generalize from specific events to create universal analogues for individual ambitions and ideals. Instead, they excerpt, copy, or translate existing figurative information (in such readily recognizable forms as news photographs or examples from art history) in order to recontextualize and question what is, at the close of the twentieth century, our thoroughly confused sense of aesthetic and ethical values. By refashioning evidence of the past, acknowledging the fragmented edifice of chronological accumulation that now confronts us, these artists hope to speak to the present or project an example for the

16

future. Rooted in the rapidly changing politics of gender roles and racial stereotypes or formulated in terms of psychological mythologies that generate examples of both human type and prototype, their work seeks to establish a collective identity from the individualism that is both the promise and the burden of contemporary American life.

Leon Golub, Manuel Ocampo, Robert Colescott, and Kerry James Marshall explicitly convey the tension inherent in the current social construct. Leon Golub's most recent work no longer engages figures in explicit positions of confrontation, alienation, or control; instead, his large figures on unstretched linen address deeper questions about the oblique, ambiguous, and intertwined relationships between such basic opposites as wealth and poverty, power and subjugation. In *Agent Orange*, 1993, the corrosiveness of chemical warfare serves as a vivid metaphor for the more insidious effects of societal dissolution. Two men and a dog, arrayed in enigmatic gestures of detachment, occupy one level of the painting; a sketchily outlined depiction of a woman disrobing floats above them. She, in turn, is held in the sights of a gun that enters from the left edge of the canvas. Golub is keenly aware of the problems inherent in depictions of broad cultural paradigms: stenciled into his field is the question "Will allegory kill art?" He solves this problem by individualizing his subject matter, making pictures culled from magazines and newspapers his own through an intensive process of painting, sanding, and scraping. His hand-tooled figures thus lose the distanced impersonality of photomechanical reproduction. Belying their mass-media origins, they project instead an imposing, emotionally

MANUEL OCAMPO
Duro es el Paso, 1992
Oil on linen
Diptych, 96 x 96
(243.8 x 243.8 cm)
Private Collection, Los Angeles;
Courtesy Fred Hoffman Fine Art,
Los Angeles

expressive physicality.

The cumulative effect of Manuel Ocampo's narratives is a slow, simmering anxiety. Ironically, Ocampo's beautifully painted canvases concentrate on the macabre aspects of humanity; they are further complicated by his choice of a traditional approach to representation that is indebted to his early artistic training with Catholic icon painters in his native Philippines. Omnipresent in the artist's work is the anger of an out-

LEON GOLUB
Agent Orange, 1993
Acrylic on linen
56 x 88 (142.2 x 223.5 cm)
Courtesy of the artist and
Josh Baer Gallery, New York

sider. Ocampo, who now lives in Los Angeles, has developed "a collage aesthetic, like living in a place with no history."[3] Mixing and matching several distinct painting styles and dialects as diverse as Spanish, French, Tagalog, and Sanskrit, he presents history as a fictive construct. This complex view is clear in *Duro es el Paso*, 1992; far from projecting a colonial imperative, the artist's gruesome encounter is seen from the perspective of the natives, who wreak their revenge on a colonial intruder. Ocampo's incorporation of text—a heraldic, bannered inscription that hovers above the scene, and the painting's title set into

17

the road that runs by a colonial out-post—powerfully reinforce the artist's sardonic take on the corrosive effects of imperialism.[4]

Inspired by artistic masterpieces and cartoon iconography, Robert Colescott's painterly compositions are structured in layers to achieve what he describes as "barrel-house cubism."[5] Fusing musical and visual notions of time into his own unique conception of physical scale, Colescott syncopates and juxtaposes related figurative vignettes across his canvases. Unified by bridge areas of pure color, his cast of characters occupy a shallow, nonperspectival space in which the real and the fantastic collide in a the-atrical, circuslike atmosphere. In *The Atom Bomb in L.A. (Do the Hula-Hula)*, 1992, Colescott takes the 1992 Los Angeles riots as a jumping-off point for a soliloquy on a broad tapestry of issues related to our urban culture of haves and have-nots, especially stereotypes of poverty, sexuality, race, and class.[6] Colescott does not propose solutions; he has noted, in fact, that "the questions are always more interesting than the answers."[7] Bringing the unwieldy dimen-sions of social, political, and philosophi-cal problems closer to the personal level of experience, Colescott's pictures get under our skin, prodding us to recognize the subtexts and consequences of our often unthinking behavior.

Flatly painted with a foreshortened perspective, Kerry James Marshall's figu-rative tableaux create a suggestive, cine-matic atmosphere for the artist's alle-gories, which slowly reveal content through ambiguity and irony. In *AKA Li'l Bit*, 1993, a young girl, presented as an icon of innocence, is circumscribed by the definitive acronym *AKA*, which projects an aura of illegality or personal subterfuge. Marshall's highly evocative rendering of this invented character's facial features is counterbalanced by the more expression-

ROBERT COLESCOTT
The Atom Bomb in L.A.
(Do the Hula-Hula), 1992
Acrylic on canvas
84 x 72 (213 .4 x 182.9 cm)
Courtesy of Phyllis Kind Gallery,
New York and Chicago

istic brush-work, drips, and other abstract passages that surround her, heightening distinctions between internal and exter-nal realities. Establishing a lexicon of symbolism, *The Lost Boys*, 1993, offers poignant portrayals of personalities that society often rejects as unimportant. The large-scale centerpiece of Marshall's series is a modern-day fairy tale of lost potential, where children learn the ways of death instead of the skills of life. The artist stations his youthful protagonists in an artificial landscape, a fantasy theme park where for a dollar one can ride a power car to nowhere and where toy guns are the aggressive symbols of triumph that anticipate the limited roles these boys can expect to be assigned as they attain adulthood.

KERRY JAMES MARSHALL
The Lost Boys,
AKA Li'l Bit, 1993
Acrylic on paper
26½ x 26½ (67.3 x 67.3 cm)
Courtesy of Madeline Murphy Rabb,
Los Angeles

Nancy Spero, Dotty Attie, Ken Aptekar, and Catherine Howe contrast idealized and real-world versions of masculine and feminine. Recasting appropriated images, often in combination with texts, they describe changing attitudes about gender through the prism of art and history. Over her long career, Nancy Spero has distilled an abundant repertoire of archetypal representations of femininity that are rooted in both ancient examples and decidedly modern prototypes. Spero's feminism eschews aggressive militancy in favor of seduction and suggestion: her conglomerate images lure us into a densely layered world of philosophical speculation. From her far-reaching pantheon of subject matter, she fashions an expansive world of possibilities for the feminine, replete with a wealth of emotional and intellectual power. In *Lilith*, 1992, she adroitly collages a mythological icon of the Hebrew *Ur*-female with a more contemporary, androgynous version of this same social archetype. Spero's females do not dictate attitudes so much as pose questions. Is the pose of androgyny a masculine surface under which lies a highly sensual female presence? Or is this figure a representation of the "male gaze" that has the

power to objectify and ultimately diminish the confidence of a powerful, mythological goddess? What finally coalesces from Spero's variegated models is a solidly unified spectrum of femininity that replaces recorded stereotype with a sweeping rereading of the role of women.

Dotty Attie has long been fascinated by the ways we order our existence through arbitrarily assigned societal roles. Throughout her career, Attie has proceeded as a scientist, scrutinizing minute details in search of clues to how this evidence, writ large, can change our perception of the world. Attie looks at the figure through the lens of renowned master painters; altering our understanding of their work, she suggests how our approach to sexuality derives from historic precedents such as the examples set forth in nineteenth-century painting. Dissecting the complex hierarchies, subtexts, and allusions bred into Gustave Courbet's "pornographic" *The Origin of The World*, 1866, she contrasts this image with specific details from Courbet's repertoire within isolated gridded panel sections in *Mixed Metaphors*, 1993. A similarly broad panoply of meaning is teased out of the fragments of Courbet's oeuvre in *After Courbet*, 1993. Adopting the artistic invention of a well-known artist almost as an alter ego, Attie is after the essence of sexual, psychological, or historical significance. In this sense, her work is not allegorical, but a decidedly of-the-moment exploration of how knowledge can affect the status of societal signifiers.

Adopting the ideal of maleness represented by old masters such as Rembrandt and Raphael, Ken Aptekar incorporates biography and autobiography into his painted interpretations of artistic icons in order to reevaluate some of our most potent presumptions about the nature of authorship. Phrases and word combinations etched in glass hover over his images, so that we comprehend his multilayered art both cognitively and visually. In *Pink Frick*, 1993, Aptekar has dramatically altered how we apprehend the established perspective on Rembrandt's

DOTTY ATTIE
After Courbet (detail), 1993
Oil on canvas
63 panels, 6 x 6 each
(15.2 x 15.2 cm); 44 x 56
(111.8 x 142.4 cm) overall
Courtesy of the artist and
P.P.O.W., New York

NANCY SPERO
Lilith, 1992
Handprinting and printed
collage on paper
46 x 19½ (116.8 x 49.5 cm)
Courtesy of the artist and
Josh Baer Gallery, New York

19

life and work, redefining one of his self-portraits in terms of the painting's condition of ownership instead of through the identity of the artist. In *Heavy Equipment*, 1992, he has arbitrarily joined the sitters of two separate Rembrandt portraits, lovingly rendering the materialistic details of the couple's clothing while omitting the declaration of identity their faces would provide.[8] The superimposed phrases, excerpts from marriage announcements published in *The New York Times*, emphasize worldly achievement, paralleling the opulence of the sitters' accoutrements. This combination of image and text implies a continuity of past and present materialist world views.

KEN APTEKAR
Heavy Equipment, 1992
Oil on wood, sandblasted glass, bolts
Diptych, 30 x 60 (76.2 x 152.4 cm)
Klinger-Gal Collection

20

Catherine Howe's idealized women reframe the aggregate of art history within a decidedly contemporary point of view. Her heroic portraits, borrowed or generalized from such prominent nineteenth- and early twentieth-century American artists as John Singer Sargent (1856–1925) and James Chapin (1887–1975), are set against backgrounds that emulate the pantheon of classic postwar abstraction created and promulgated by painters such as Clyfford Still (1904–1980)

and Willem de Kooning (b. 1904). In *The Web*, 1992, a haughty grande dame straight out of a Sargent portrait does not reside in a society setting, but, as if existing outside of time, literally emerges from a thick de Kooning-esque soup of paint gobs and brushstrokes. Howe has successfully hybridized these two dissimilar styles, staging a collision of seemingly dissonant elements within a single perspective. Recognizing the brashness of her appropriations, she imbues her pictures with a subtle sense of humor. Howe does not borrow surface appearances arbitrarily: playing upon the cultural meanings surrounding these styles, she proposes a terrain where representations of women interrupt and "tame" the expansiveness of what is perhaps the most distinctly masculine school of American painting.

Immigrants to the United States, Luis Cruz Azaceta and Hung Liu mine their unique personal histories as transplanted outsiders thrust into American culture. Throughout his career Luis Cruz Azaceta has explored issues of cultural displacement, often through autobiographical self-portraiture that enlarges his physical countenance into that of a symbolic everyman who tries to make sense of a blank, abstract world and who, through his actions, broadens specific events into metaphors for the human condition. Recently, he has begun to use a reductive, aqueous technique to provide an urgent, breathless immediacy in his assessments of his progress or failures of assimilation as he changes his setting (from Cuba to New York as a student and,

CATHERINE HOWE
The Web, 1992
Oil on canvas
82 x 58 (208.3 x 147.3 cm)
Rubell Family Collections,
New York

recently, to New Orleans). Presented against the backdrop of a flattened plane, his figures interact but rarely overlap. Instead, they exist as discrete integers floating in unmarked landscapes. In *Tchoupitoulas Shoot Out*, 1992, the artist explores another kind of displacement, that of neighborhood violence. His figures are portrayed in broad strokes—almost reduced to animalistic shapes—that amplify his condemnation of the abdication of responsibility that accompanies violent action. Emblematic of the isolation we experience in our everyday interactions, his streamlined figures are ferocious in their archetypal intensity.

LUIS CRUZ AZACETA
Tchoupitoulas Shoot Out, 1992
Acrylic and Polaroids on canvas
120 x 120 (304.8 x 304.8 cm)
Courtesy of Frumkin/Adams Gallery, New York

As a student during the Chinese Cultural Revolution, Hung Liu journeyed through the Communist system of rigidly appropriate behavior and education; the rupture she experienced upon her subsequent immigration to the United States is at the heart of her work. Liu constructs intensely theatrical spaces in which her figures embody the collision of past and present inherent in the changing roles of women in both Eastern and Western cultures. *Swan Song*, 1992, is a visual essay on cultural displacement that combines fragmentary glimpses of Chinese women taken from historical sources with an aria from a Cultural Revolution-era opera. Liu's images of these women are isolated in ovals that assert the distanced sensibility of miniature portraits; they are further isolated by their setting within the opera's text, which is written in Western-style musical notation and phonetic language instead of the Chinese alphabet. These portraits are counterbalanced by inset cutouts of aggresive dancers who, ironically, represent both

aesthetic beauty and the patriotic anti-intellectualism ruthlessly enforced by the Cultural Revolution. Liu's layered work embodies the artist's understanding of the contradiction between reality and highly charged or even authoritarian representations that purport to convey an absolute reality.

* * *

HUNG LIU
Swan Song, 1993
Oil on canvas and mixed media
61 x 91⅝ x 3
(154.9 x 232.7 x 7.6 cm)
Courtesy of Rena Bransten Gallery, San Francisco

Mythical figures live many lives, die many deaths, and in this they differ from the characters we find in novels, who can never go beyond the single gesture. But in each of these lives and deaths all the others are present, and we can hear their echo. Only when we become aware of a sudden consistency between incompatibles can we say we have crossed the threshold of myth.

—Roberto Calasso[9]

Psychological or philosophical gestures provide the impetus for the paintings of Donald Baechler, Drew Beattie & Daniel Davidson, Phyllis Bramson, Michael Byron, Inga Frick, David Humphrey, Jim Lutes, Melissa Miller, and Deborah Oropallo, for whom the predominantly social implications of bodily representation are phrased in mythological terms. Some plumb the traditions of Modernism, incorporating the archetypes of Freudian thought, or use other literary sources, such as fairy tales and nursery rhymes, to create analogies for the subconscious; others create their own hybridized versions of idealized humanity. Rooted in an interactive, collage-based approach to image making, their pictures dramatize the human condition by attempting to find ways to envision it as if for the first time. For most of these artists, language is of secondary importance to imagistic shards that are imbued with the qualities and characteristics of personality.

Ida Applebroog, Charles Garabedian, Melissa Miller, and Deborah Oropallo craft an elegant painterly skin, but beneath their opulent surfaces lurk provocative, often intensely probing questions about human nature. Ida Applebroog's paintings linger somewhere between a bright childhood fantasy and the darkness of a nightmare vision; in her work flowers, birds, and animals can go suddenly wild, and formerly friendly acquaintances can quickly turn into ominous strangers who

22

reveal their darker undersides. Recently, she has explored fairy tales. Inverting the childhood morals they contain, she uses them to show how interrupted innocence can alter the future terms of intimate personal interaction. Applebroog, who has commented that "I never make benign images,"[10] takes as her starting point emblems of personal or social disorder. She embeds these fragments in serial vignettes rendered in a combination of highly polished, tonal realism and a deliberately childlike illustrative style. Increasingly, she also moves painting off

IDA APPLEBROOG
Empty Orchestra (detail), 1993
Dimensions variable
Courtesy of Ronald Feldman
Fine Arts, New York

the wall, fashioning room-sized installations comprised of both free-standing and wall-mounted canvases. Applebroog's psychological exposés are neither distanced nor linear: instead of maintaining a safe distance between viewer and object, she liberates the commonly accepted conceit of paint on canvas as a surrogate picture window, creating instead a forest of images into which the viewer literally enters and becomes an integral participant.

Charles Garabedian's series *Study for the Iliad* questions, challenges, and mutates Homer's epic themes into a meditation on the foibles of twentieth-century cultural development and technological advancement. Garabedian's interest in the *Iliad* derives from his initial response to reading it: "I saw it as a bloody, crazy thing in which the poetry is in praise of rape, murder, thievery, lying, cheating, plundering. There are no specifics, no real personages."[11] Nevertheless, Garabedian's painterly vision is expressed with ironic humor and imbued with a luminosity that contradicts the bloody actions he depicts. Applying his paint in thin layers, he meticulously delineates figures that seem possessed by an internal light. These ambiguous characters seem to exist in another time and place, outside reality and, despite their gruesome wounds, beyond harm. Like actors in a Noh play, they convey in their stylized poses a set of moral values. From this distanced realism emerges an allegorical study that constructs verities capable of existing only outside normative parameters. Expanding the fertile references already available in this archaic epic, Garabedian's vision of Homer's encompassing narrative is, above all, couched in terms that are compellingly universal.

Man and the inhabitants of nature become synonymous in the landscapes of Melissa Miller. In her early work, animals often stood as surrogates for human beings; recently, she has shifted the framework of her painted scenarios to "express a more internal focus" where "animals, humans, and humanoids address issues of the human psyche."[12] In Miller's fantastic visions, people are caught in a continuous state of transformation. In *The Temptation of Saint Anthony*, 1993, her version of the biblical story is inspired by Gustave Flaubert's 1874 retelling of Saint Anthony's torment. Miller manifests the prophet's spiritual transformation through a stylized melange evocative of the magical realism of Latino and Indian cultures in her native South Texas as well as the phantasmagoric inventions that haunt the religious allegories of apocalyptic Dutch and Flemish painters such as Hieronymus Bosch (c. 1450–1516) and Pieter Bruegel the Elder (c. 1525–1569). Ghosts and demons, as well as other dark and positive forces drawn from art-historical, literary, or biblical sources, populate this picture, but despite their fantastic attributes,

Miller's creatures always symbolize the inner struggles that accompany the process of transformation.

Deborah Oropallo's lexicon of images is derived from instruments of learning: the stuff of fairy tales, fables, and instruction manuals is enfolded into her painterly process, becoming either the topic of poetic improvisation or a rigorously reproduced icon of authority. Teetering between the real and the remembered, Oropallo's introspective pictures adopt and personify archetypes in order to describe the pervasive impact of memory on perception. Texts, often interspersed

in her work, provoke the powerful resonance of an alphabet lament in *The Woodsman*, 1993, and biting social critique, articulated in the didactic syntax of a police instruction manual, in *Three-Man Patrol*, 1993. Unlike Pop icons, her juxtapositions of image and text are intended to be read and digested over time instead of comprehended with a glance. Oropallo's canvases are structured more as musical scores than as prose texts or newspaper reportage; her overlapping layers of

23

translucent glazes and painted words fuse into a fugue-like composition that constantly shifts between the artist's own psychological states and her awareness of larger social issues.

Kim Dingle, Elena Sisto, and Carole Caroompas propose contemporary myths based on their own invented heroes and rogues. Kim Dingle's monumental portraits simultaneously display ominous, sardonic, and comic tendencies. Her quirky pictures are emboldened by a sense of black humor that undermines the pure ideals of feminine daintiness just as certainly as it compromises macho aggressiveness. In *Girl Boxing*, 1992, she subverts our understanding of the accepted conventions of the brutal, masculine sport of boxing by dressing her combatants in the accoutrements of female innocence and purity— frilly dresses and patent-leather shoes. Her little girls in party dresses operate in a world remote from the realms of responsibility; completely free from the societal strictures of adulthood, they play out their creator's fantasies, even though their

sparring activities reflect fantasies of power and maturity that foreshadow adult behavior. Whether depicted roaming in packs across a vast, bucolic landscape or pictured in dramatic one-on-one confrontations, Dingle's girls always manage to resurrect from the ashes of life's absurdities a strong, cognitive sense of the value of individual identity.

In Elena Sisto's strategy, the limitations of graphic representation are mitigated and undercut by abstraction, which bridges real world activities and internalized fantasy. Sisto's explorations of the struggles of feminine self-awareness are described by cartoon symbols, figures

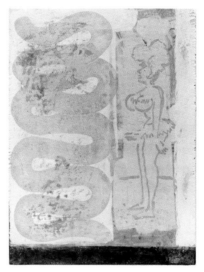

that she uses as a device to distance herself from the intimacies of her personal coming of age and to refract a singular icon into the myriad interpretations that society confers on female identity. Her intimately scaled paintings are painstakingly crafted, with pastel colors and translucent overlays of tempera paint that diffuse the aggressive, overtly charged subject matter they contain. Sisto's main heroine in this work is the classic blond bombshell, a Barbie doll of a woman who has been the staple of cheap movies, cocktail napkin jokes, and girlie magazines. Chronically depicted as the unwitting victim of the leering male gaze, these scantily clad figures also represent, for the artist, a precursor to female consciousness. Through a painterly process

24

of recontextualization, Sisto's bimbo evolves into a new Eve who, shedding negative connotations, stands on the threshold of power and confidence.

Carole Caroompas's series *Before and After Frankenstein: The Woman Who Knew Too Much* alludes to Mary Shelley and her literary invention of the "reconstructed" man in order to question the myth of the oppositional nature of femininity and artistic creativity, and to emphasize the contemporary shift from the body as personal territory to the body as social metaphor. Each painting in this series becomes a chapter in Caroompas's narration of the conflict between the sexes, which she sees as a perpetual battle that plays itself out in every aspect of our lives. In *Before and After Frankenstein: The Woman Who Knew Too Much: Specter and Emanation*, 1993, Caroompas presents two images that simultaneously reinforce and reject each other. Luridly colored, provocatively insipid scenes of a stereotypically "fun" male-female interaction, repeated like wallpaper, form the painting's backdrop. Derived from a photograph, an image of a couple unhappily sitting back-to-back is the painting's central focus; this more verisimilitudinous pair is everything that the happy, completely superficial cartoon duo is not. In Caroompas's off-balance epics, natural reality always clashes with the ridiculous, often-nightmarish simplemindedness of some of our basic assumptions about culture and society.

Hybrid, often highly fragmentary figures populate the paintings of Phyllis Bramson, Michael Byron, and Donald Baechler. Phyllis Bramson breaks up her picture plane, constructing a storyboard-like narrative whose parts coalesce into a unified thematic focus regarding the vicissitudes of sensual experience. Isolated, her disjointed images stand as snapshots of the varieties of the condition of being. Together, they provoke a disquieting anxiety that is at least partially derived from her unsettling, even jarring juxtapositions, which use collage techniques to combine excerpts from mass-produced, store-bought paintings with her own deftly realized vignettes. Bramson often incorporates a clown—that quintessential symbol of the dichotomy between surface appearance and the psyche—as a moral agent who bears witness. In *Broken Cup*, 1992, we see disembodied figurative passages—a crying child, the shoulder and partially exposed breast of a woman, a man with a bird's nest on his head and a branch growing from his mouth, a foot with a branch sprouting from the sole, the top of a clown's head—interspersed with similar excerpts of landscapes and still lifes. Bramson's amalgam does not follow a linear narrative, but instead summons the larger lexicon of life, in which sense

CAROLE CAROOMPAS
Before and After Frankenstein:
The Woman Who Knew Too Much:
Spectre and Emanation, 1993
Acrylic on canvas
60 x 48 (152.4 x 73.9 cm)
Courtesy of Sue Spaid Fine Art,
Los Angeles

PHYLLIS BRAMSON
Broken Cup, 1991–92
Mixed media and oil on canvas
72 x 48 (121.9 x 182.9 cm)
Courtesy of Brody's Gallery,
Washington, D.C. and
Phyllis Kind Gallery,
Chicago and New York

and sensibility is but a part of the individual nature of emotions and understanding.

Michael Byron's eclectic melange of pictures and epigrammatic texts subject the intuitive act of perception to analytic scrutiny. Byron's compositional structure signals that his paintings are fictional narratives peopled with mysterious figures, while his accompanying texts often propose philosophical conundrums that question the actions of his characters. Unlike many of the textual strategies used by artists in this exhibition, Byron's phrases ask us to reevaluate how we choose to read a picture—and by implication, how we choose to understand reality. The philosophical affinities between the accepted meanings of his depictions and his seemingly non-sequitur slogans— "people sit and watch" or "people sit and worry"—create a double entendre that equates his formalized depictions of theatrical activities with the more modern, more psychologically aware, ideas that underpin contemporary performance art. Borrowed from the terminology of theatrics, these quotidian axioms are expressed in the thoroughly nostalgic vocabulary of nineteenth-century illustrations. Combining past styles with present attitudes, Byron establishes visual conundrums that question the malleability of societal rules.

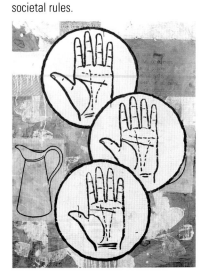

Donald Baechler's cartoonish appendages and organs are not connected to corporeal bodies; rather, they appear as out-

lines lacking the distinctions of personality. As such, they are blank slates upon which new codes can be written. Signifiers of the mind-body schism, Baechler's depersonalized heads and hands are dispassionately rendered with an iconic primitivism that is simultaneously compelling and sinister. Overpainted on collage fragments scavenged from many sources, his drawings suggest an admixture of generic bodily consciousness and intimate sensuality. The hands in *Three Palms*, 1992, confidently claim the right to the unknown future predicted in their lifelines; they suggest infinite possibilities that are echoed in Baechler's constructed fields, where multitudinous overlays of information produced by many anonymous hands reveals, almost like pentimenti, remembered fragments of past experience. This compelling compendium of travel receipts, calendars from distant places, personal notes, and children's homework assignments, meshed together with Baechler's reductive imagery, has the cumulative effect of a disruption of reality that, like a sudden shock, offers the possibility of a return to innocence.

The focus on the head as the locus for both intellectual and emotional content is found in varying degrees in the work of Jim Lutes, David Humphrey, and Inga Frick, as well as the team efforts of Drew Beattie & Daniel Davidson. But whether speculating about the nature of individuality in the context of multiple perspectives or exploding the conceits of portraiture, these artists consistently contrast

MICHAEL BYRON
People Sit and Wait (Birth of Performance Art), 1993
Oil and collage on canvas
27½ x 39⅜ (69.8 x 99.9 cm)
Courtesy of Galerie Philippe Gravier, Paris

DONALD BAECHLER
Three Palms, 1992
Gesso, gouache, collage and coffee on paper
53 x 40½ (134.6 x 102.9 cm)
Courtesy of Sperone Westwater Gallery, New York

notions of invented reality with conceptions of authenticity. Although Jim Lutes's reductive figuration deepens the psychological complexity broached in the late work of Philip Guston, Lutes's terrain of interrupted individual description is perhaps best viewed as a departure from the classical perspective of self-portraiture. It is as if the artist, spinning out variations on the theme of self, is trying to find a flexible framework for self-portraiture that will accommodate both his everyday experience and the territory of art history. In *Tire Party*, 1992, a recognizable outline only slowly emerges from the thick tangle of expressionistic brushwork that covers the canvas. Lutes's sensual paint application manifests the puzzle of the mind-body division in terms of the split between idealized and referential gestures that has dominated the vernacular of postwar American art. But nightmarish memories and brooding meditations on morality lurk just below the lushly painted surfaces of his disembodied heads. Lutes's command of the language of painterly expression is rooted in an intuitive response that relates

both to actual place and the subconscious. His creative endeavors describe the root of individualism as a process of self-awareness that can only be activated through communications that are phrased in both specific and universal terms.

Drew Beattie & Daniel Davidson use four hands to make a painting, and they employ a number of distancing devices to

orchestrate this multitude in the service of what is usually a solitary activity. Instead of creating a direct record of how the hand of the artist shapes and humanizes his content, this collaborative team employs technological devices that essentially remove the traditional, tactile presence of the author's hand. Their paintings are not created additively, brushstroke by brushstroke; instead, plow, scrape, and drag marks are incised into the painting's field through the use of remote-controlled toy cars and voice-activated trucks. Driven across the surface of the canvas, these devices effectively disconnect initial intentions from eventual outcomes. Beattie & Davidson's heads are neither male nor female, and thus sidestep any positive or negative associations ascribed to gender. Instead, their portrait amalgams attract or repel depending on how closely they approximate or deviate from our own idealized norms. What emerges in *Dumb Wonder*, 1993, or *Call Me Fantastic*, 1993, is an admixture of accident and control that, like a Rorschach inkblot, gains its content not from the hand of the creator, but from the values and beliefs recognized and maintained by the viewer.

Working with a computerized system of magnification, elongation, and compression, David Humphrey subtly alters, exaggerates, or decomposes photographs of his parents' wedding, effectively neutralizing their validity as factual records of 1950s prosperity and family stability.

JIM LUTES
Tire Party, 1992
Acrylic on linen
57 x 69 (144.8 x 175.3 cm)
Collection Edie and
James Cloonan, Chicago

27

DREW BEATTIE & DANIEL DAVIDSON
Call Me Fantastic, 1992
Oil on canvas
96 x 74 (243.8 x 187.96 cm)
Courtesy of Gallery Paule Anglim,
San Francisco

Further disrupting their status as evidential records, he inserts images culled from comic books and other outlets of popular culture. Humphrey has remarked that "images are the end product of cultural life."[13] Through his processes, he refocuses our attention away from the actuality of the depicted narrative and toward the cumulative function of memory. In *Guest*, 1993, the monumental portrait of a young woman is presented out of focus, her eyes, nose, and mouth each repeated twice, as if captured by slow-motion photography. Two very disparate elements are superimposed over this portrait. Dripped and splattered paint recalls the aggressive, even hubristic expressionism of postwar, New York School painters; this clashes head-on with a fifties-style illustration of a woman's hairstyle. Creating a repertoire of invented, imagined, and factual elements, Humphrey fashions a deeply personal, highly evocative, but fictional "portrait" of an event that, while critically important to his life, existed independently of his own experiences.

Inga Frick layers images one over another, evoking a dreamlike state in which cognitive functions merge with the cacophony of the subconscious. Frick has a passion for the immaterial; for her, the ephemera of the physical world acts as a doorway to the metaphysical, and the fragmented imagery that populates her painting supports a variety of meanings. Her cool approach to process and content

is delineated through her use of illustrated fabric as a grounding field over which photograph-based images are constructed. In *Black and White and Read All Over*, 1992, Frick builds translucent layers on a ready-made ground of commercially produced, flatly rendered nursery-rhyme illustrations, provoking a vigorous compositional tension between the field and the objects set within it. The flashes of phenomenological experience—a mysterious, fragmentary vision of someone riding a bicycle, or, as in *Black and White and Read All Over*, an almost imperceptible female form that emerges from the commotion of the fabric background—become threads in a dense visual tapestry. Whether approximating reality or imagination, these associations stimulate the viewer's own contemplations on the relative nature of past and present, imagination and reality.

* * *

INGA FRICK
Black and White and Read All Over (detail), 1992
Acrylic on fabric
Triptych, 76¾ x 211¼
(194.9 x 536.6 cm)
Courtesy of Jones Troyer Fitzpatrick Gallery,

DAVID HUMPHREY
Guest, 1993
Oil on canvas
72 x 56 (182.9 x 142.24 cm)
Courtesy of McKee Gallery,
New York

Everything is related to the body, as if it had just been rediscovered after being long forgotten; body image, body language, body consciousness, liberation of the body are the pass-words.

—Jean Starobinski,
"The Natural and Literary History of Bodily Sensation"[14]

Our bodies are with us, though we have always had trouble saying ex-actly how. We are, in various con-ceptions or metaphors, in our body, or having a body, or at one with our body, or alienated from it. The body is both ourselves and other, and as such the object of emotions from love to disgust.

—Peter Brooks,
"Narrative and the Body"[15]

Representations of the body in contempo-rary art serve two purposes. On the one hand, they establish connections between our internalized perceptions and the external realities of our social conditions. On the other hand, generic, broadly as-sociative figures allow artists to construct compelling equations for how individuality is increasingly defined in terms of accep-tance to or rebellion from a group dynam-ic. Contextualizing the human figure with-in the framework of sociological, political, or psychological activities, the artists in this exhibition create images that provide us with a means of navigating the irra-tional subtexts of our outwardly rational existence.

We tell ourselves stories in order to create a framework for our lives, and to locate ourselves physically and spiritually by giving our body narrative markers that make it recognizable. Narratives about the body were a central preoccupation in American and European nineteenth-century literature; the visual arts also focused on the body as a way to unravel the web of tangled impetuses of religion and materialism through the objective scrutiny of realism. More than a century

later, the authority of representational descriptions has, necessarily, given way to a more metaphoric tactic, where the body signifies myriad meanings that, while distinct from the materialistic world-view of realism, remain deeply rooted in humanism. Within the past several years writers as diverse as Jeanette Winterson (*Written on the Body*) and Susan Sontag (*The Collector*), as well as film-makers such as Peter Greenaway (*Prospero's Books*), and Sally Potter (*Orlando*), have developed hybrid figurative systems. Their transitional forms, hovering be-tween reality and metaphor, mark the body as the key element in an otherwise abstract arena of multivalent experiences.

In a similar sense, each of the artists participating in this exhibition recognizes that the act of painting retains its viability only when it is asserted as an optimistic gesture capable of incorporating such tra-ditional ideas as allegory and myth with-out negating the fundamental transforma-tions—positive and negative—that have marked the progress of the twentieth cen-tury. While age-old constructs, the con-ventions of allegory and myth that these artists employ can be seen as an exten-sion of the schism between idealized and referential gestures that has dominated the vernacular of postwar American art. After a century of modernist invention, their art asserts that representations gain power only when they proffer commu-nicative gestures capable of incorporating the past even while they seek to create their own distinctive future. In this sense, their artistic endeavors maintain an al-most utopian desire to affect change by holding the painterly mirror to reality.

NOTES

1. Jeanette Winterson, *Written on the Body* (New York: Alfred A. Knopf, 1993), 89.

2. Leon Golub, interview with Lilly Wei, "On Nationality: 13 Artists," *Art in America* (September 1991), 124.

3. Manuel Ocampo, interview with the author, April 1993.

4. The bannered text reads, "El hombre justo la muerte del justo, la muerte del pecador el hombre pecador" (The just man, the death of the just man, the sinner's death, the sinner); the title, Duro es el Paso, translates as "hard is the way."

5. Robert Colescott, interview with the author, March 1993.

6. The painting's title makes reference to three days of rioting that began in the South Central district of Los Angeles in April 1992 as a result of the acquittal of white policemen in a trial alleging police brutality against Rodney King, a black suspect.

7. Robert Colescott, interview with the author, March 1993.

8. The two Rembrandt paintings Aptekar marries are *Portrait of Maerten Day*, 1634 (left), and *Portrait of Machteld van Doorn*, 1634 (right).

9. Roberto Calasso, *The Marriage of Cadmus and Harmony* (New York: Alfred A. Knopf, 1993), 22.

10. Ida Applebroog, interview with Karen Michele, National Public Radio, June 19, 1993.

11. Charles Garabedian, interview with Miles Beller, *Artweek* (April 23, 1992), 15.

12. Melissa Miller, letter to the author, March 10, 1992.

13. David Humphrey, "The Abject Romance of Low Resolution," *Lusitania* no. 4 (1993), 155.

14. Jean Starobinski, "The Natural and Literary History of Bodily Sensation," in *Fragments for a History of the Human Body*, Part Two, Michael Feher, ed. (New York: Zone, 1989), 353.

15. Peter Brooks, "Narrative and the Body," in *Body Work: Objects of Desire in Modern Narrative* (Cambridge, Massachusetts and London: Harvard University Press, 1993), 1.

NOTE TO THE READER

Measurements of artworks are provided through-out in inches, followed by centimeters in paren-theses. Height precedes width, which precedes depth.

Entries have been arranged alphabetically by artist. Essays have been written by:

Maia Damianovic, independent art critic, New York

Judith Russi Kirshner, Director, School of Art and Design, The University of Illinois at Chicago

Klaus Ottmann, Curator of Exhibitions, Wesleyan University, Middletown, Connecticut

David Pagel, independent art critic, Los Angeles and New York

Maria Porges, artist and independent art critic, Oakland, California

Marla Price, Director, Modern Art Museum of Ft. Worth

Gary Sangster, Executive Director, Cleveland Center for Contemporary Art

Lowery Stokes Sims, Associate Curator of Twentieth Century Art, Metropolitan Museum of Art

Alisa Tager, writer, New York and Los Angeles

While it may seem a bit far-fetched to use a reference to television synthiotics to describe the work of Ida Applebroog, the analogy is apt. In the same way that Bruce Warner and Oliver Stone, in the

I D A   A P P L E B R O O G

miniseries "Wild Palms,"[1] used images that actually intruded into the space of the viewer—Applebroog in recent showings has brought the canvas off the wall and into our space. It is a bold gesture which shatters the illusionary ruse of easel painting and the hegemony of the wall as the exclusive siting of this hierarchical prestidigitation.

Painting's intrusion into the viewer's space is all the more disconcerting because Applebroog has not in any way modified painting's means of presentation. Individual canvases, mounted on deep-boxed stretchers, hang on the wall, lean against the wall, or are emphatically bolted to the floor, with stretchers, nails, and frayed canvas edges in full view. Thus our spatial relationship with painting—conventionally defined at eye level—is recast as our perspective shifts from wall referent to the floor.

These undisguised deceits are typical of Applebroog's work, another form of the intense deconstruction that has characterized her art over the last three decades. Although she is part of a generation that came to maturity thirty years ago, her work has over the last decade been readily contextualized within that of a younger generation of artists, who found in her seemingly disjointed revelations of secret states of being a sympathetic mind. Psychological, as well as physical abuse; medical incompetence and dysfunction; personal torment and disequilibrium; deformity and pretense of normalcy; intimate exploitation and whole holocausts; all are fodder for political

appropriateness prescribed by recent theoretical constructs.

Applebroog's images force us to admit that they are often enacted in circumstances deemed 'normal' and even 'civilized.' As Thomas Sokolowski has noted, in Applebroog's world we are confronted with an on-going soap opera.[2] The irony is that through the vehicles of serial novellas, talk television (Oprah, Montel, Geraldo, Jane, Joan, Sally, and Phil), and the 'reality' of reenacted television ("Cops," "Unsolved Mysteries"), the tragedies of life—real and perceived—have been so trivialized as to be rendered meaningless and without validity. It is with a strange sense of reassurance that we can confront them in Applebroog's work, in her cool, monochrome palette, translucent surfaces, and somehow reconnect with life's pungent seriousness.

LOWERY STOKES SIMS

Freida S., 1993
Oil on canvas
2 panels, 110 x 72
(279.4 x 182.9 cm)
Courtesy of Ronald Feldman
Fine Arts, New York

1. Bruce Warner and Oliver Stone, "Wild Palms," ABC-TV, May 16–19, 1993.

2. Thomas W. Sokolowski, "This is to show people. . .," in *Ida Applebroog: Happy Families.* With essays by Lowery S. Sims, Thomas Sokolowski, Marilyn A. Zeitlin [exh. cat., Contemporary Arts Museum, Houston: 1990]. 19.

32

There is virtually no way to recuperate written language from becoming embedded in the realm of visual culture when words are entered into paintings. The conjunction of words and images into a

K E N   A P T E K A R

single work of art creates a hybrid discourse that falls heavily on the side of vision. Ken Aptekar's intriguing constructions balance image and text seductively. Typeset words float across the pictures and reverberate before our vision, arousing interest in identifying the underlying relationship between highly disparate words and images, and how they correlate to form new, previously unknown, meanings.

Using a generic technique of bolting thick panes of glass, etched with text, to the surface of elegantly painted boards, the artist makes a multilayered object that subdues the potency of his image sources. The narrative and emotive power of historical recognition of paintings by Rembrandt and Raphael is surreptitiously evacuated in Aptekar's process of transcribing original sources in subtly fractured or obviously constricted manners. Aptekar approaches the business of transcription with a certain ironic pleasure, parodically teasing, for instance, in titling one work *And How Did That Make You Feel*, or, implying bombast, naming another *Heavy Equipment*. His resourceful method rephrases familiar paintings by inserting terse, disruptive texts into the visual field of each work that conjure a perverse dialectic of status.

The effect of a disconcerting non-sequitur is immediately evident in these works. Acutely edited and rearticulated texts pose elusive questions and forge ill-defined connectives between thoughts and very precise but discordantly fragmented musings. A self-portrait by

Rembrandt, an apostolic post-resurrection scene by Raphael, and a betrothal, again by Rembrandt, are ingeniously reframed, recolored, or recomposed to create cryptic reproductions. These 'object/paintings' spark revisions to the systematic definitions of aesthetic authority and socially constructed assumptions of power suggested by the unadorned imagery. The reductive list of alternations in *Pink Frick* plays a simple word game before a compassionate self-portrait of Rembrandt-in-pink that invites parallel readings about Rembrandt, the current location of the portrait—the Frick Museum—and the institution's philanthropic, union-busting benefactor and namesake. An insidious undercurrent of social networks of power and control is articulated through historically masculine voices of congregation, coupling, ownership, and authority. The messages appear enticingly acute, but operate fluidly in an open realm of floating signifiers, as the words drift over the surface of the picture plane. In Aptekar's frame of reference, this ambiguity suggests the residual force of history and language as lucid masculine concepts that are complacent, resistant, and potentially retaliatory, but palpably open to revision and recompilation.

GARY SANGSTER

Pink Frick, 1993
Oil on wood, bolts,
sandblasted glass
4 panels, 60 x 60
(152.4 x 152.4 cm)
Klinger-Gal Collection

34

It is barely possible to conceal the initial shock of recognition at the point of view presented in *Mixed Metaphors* or *Mixed Messages*. Isolating the most audacious fragments of troubling, notorious paint-

D O T T Y   A T T I E

ings by historical masters Courbet, Géricault, and Eakins, Dotty Attie reconfigures them into a highly ordered format that underscores the present urgency and tension of their complex psychosexual and political-personal messages. Nothing is withheld from our gaze: Attie's paintings do possess shock value, but they are not shocking; they are subtle and discrete. These are familiar images, familiar forms. Glowing comfortably in warm tones of muted browns and yellows, their even sheen camouflages the painterly control the artist exerts in her reinvention of past authority in present dilemmas.

In fact, the most striking factor of these paintings is not their subject matter, nor the matter-of-fact genitalia depicted, it is their insistence on the grid as the defining form of the logic of reproduction and representation. As with most of Attie's paintings, an extremely small scale square canvas is the dominant stylistic feature that grounds her work within the realm of the photograph. This is particularly evident in the doubly-reduced image fragments presented, in *After Courbet*, like a series of white-bordered slides on a light table. The formal order of the grid enables the artist to dismember historical imagery at will, without lapsing into nostalgic celebration of past painterly triumphs or allowing the work to collapse into visual guessing games that circulate images without valuing them.

The dark, inviting opulence of Attie's historical details is conditioned to the present by a persistent discipline of painting, where seamless, photo-like surfaces coa-

lesce into fragmented, quasi-cellular forms. Each image possesses an insistent similarity that steels our focus to all parts of the picture. Attie's composed paintings elaborate equivalence, only rarely qualifying the erasure of difference with isolated, dramatic moments of subjugation, passive gestures of surrender, or wild-eyed expressions of genuine fear.

Attie's paintings are energized with narrative possibilities and mixed messages. Nothing is certain, save the elliptical parallels of stylistic replication and historical allusion. The recognizable, reminiscent features and suggestive fragments contain the latent, aromatic quality of memory. As Courbet exposed and explored the 'origin of the world' in his terms, Attie dissects and dislocates Courbet's *The Origin of the World* as an act of tender contemplation on orders of medical, ritual, or semiotic violence against women throughout history. In her hands the nature of mortality looms presciently closer through precise, candid renderings of the visible weakness and fragility of flesh and blood. The inverse of origins, originality, and birth is the finality of ineffable closure and creative stasis. The mien of death becomes intoxicating in the end, as paintings and bodies are sliced apart and reconstructed through Attie's exacting, elegant revisions of seductive social, sexual, and power relations.

GARY SANGSTER

Mixed Metaphors, 1993

Oil on canvas
36 panels, each 6 x 6
(15.2 x 15.2 cm); 34 x 55
(86.4 x 139.7 cm) overall
Courtesy of the artist and
P.P.O.W., New York

Luis Cruz Azaceta's emotional paintings examine the way an individual can be torn asunder by internal and external tensions, and the way that society can exacerbate these strains while affecting other,

L U I S   C R U Z   A Z A C E T A

even greater horrors and indignities. For over two decades, he has painted figurative images in order to examine the violent undercurrents in society and their effects on individuals.

While Azaceta constantly changes his style and mode of expression, his ability to render emotional representations of frightening conditions and alienating circumstances has remained consistent. He has moved from a dark and impassioned expressionism, through formal abstraction, and recently has turned to a more sparsely styled figuration. With few exceptions, he has always incorporated both abstraction and figuration in his work, finding in their coexistence an acute emotional pitch. In a similar sense, Azaceta's content establishes conditions where contradictions of mode, theme, and narrative can coexist. Whether dealing with topics like urban violence, Latin American political abuses, the environment, or AIDS, he exposes and examines societal ruptures in his paintings to evoke compassion without becoming mired in moralizing or sentimentality.

Split Rafter is the continuation of a theme he has been examining for over a decade—that of the exile who has left Cuba by boat (this theme is particularly poignant for Azaceta, who left Cuba for the United States in 1960, at the age of eighteen). The title of this painting refers to a traveler who must choose between his country, his family, and his beliefs. The gaunt figure's physique reinforces the uncertain tension implicit in such a dramatic 'split.' He stands knee-deep in

water, contemplating the vessel which will carry him: that one of his hands is a hammer indicates that he has built this raft; since his other hand is an oar, he is clearly the lone sailor. His solitude is evidenced by his penetrating, yet distanced gaze, as well as the massive purple-grey circle hanging over him. A fragile grid whose whiteness belies the suffering and pain implied by the central image spans a colorfully aqueous sea, further reinforcing the existential nature of the sailor's dilemma.

While Azaceta's paintings may depict distinct moments, they are not static representations meant to convey precise information. *Tchoupitoulas Shoot Out*, where three teenage boys engage in a gunfight, is more allegory than reportage, even though Tchoupitoulas is a street, well known to Azaceta, which runs through a high crime area along the Mississippi River. Shootouts are common, but the visionary story painted by Azaceta is imaginary. Veracity and exactitude are subordinated to the artist's need to communicate an impression of anguish and terror. The scenarios he depicts are always nonspecific commentaries on conditions or situations which have enduring social and emotional ramifications. By focusing on impact instead of documentation, Azaceta pushes the realm of sentiment toward transformative perception.

ALISA TAGER

Split Rafter, 1993
Acrylic on canvas, rope
120 x 120 (304.8 x 304.8 cm)
Courtesy of Frumkin/Adams Gallery, New York

38

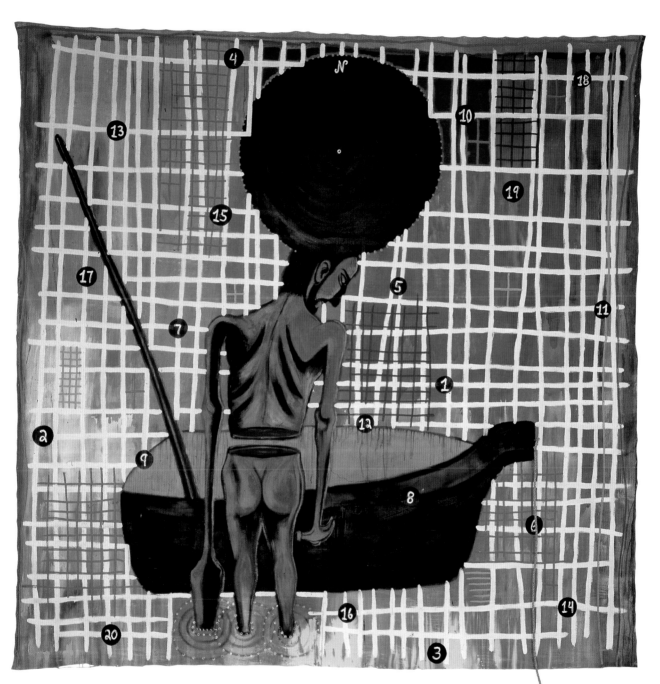

In Donald Baechler's narrative correspondences, images break down into tiny semantic particles of meaning with discrete identities capable of evoking a Proustian flood of memory. Flocks of

D O N A L D   B A E C H L E R

migratory images appear, reappear, get covered by other images, and solidify into shapes, as if seeking each other through an open cartography upon which identity is drawn and simultaneously flees. Analogous to biological germination, Baechler's fertile, painterly laminations straddle, conjugate, and traverse affiliations.

As if a presentiment of a troubled and fragmented contemporaneity, Baechler's visual intertextuality encourages a crossbred variety of identities and realities. Incorporated on the level of the readymade, the found drawings the artist collages onto the surface of his paintings intensify the historical conspicuousness of these images as archives of public consciousness. Each is a carrier of different urban traces, from "Charlie," the Hispanic-American schoolboy and his notebooks rich with social, economic, and multicultural associations, to the vaguer politics of a weathered Moroccan calendar printed in both Arabic and French, with its inherent repertoire of colonial/ imperial overtones.

Baechler's repetitive tracings of such distinct collections of images suggest a cultural still life. In *Profile With Four Palms #1*, all traces of specific features dissolve into a generic 'everyman' diagram of identity located somewhere between apparition and graffiti. The neutral contour of an eyeless, whitewashed, kabuki-like face contains the static diagrams of four hands from a standard palm reading manual. Other dominant images—beach balls, children's wooden building blocks, a water pitcher—are

repeated by the artist as randomly interchangeable pictographic templates, but their stripped and limited value as indexing signs is held in abeyance by an oceanic background of painterly references. The loose and exuberant play between traditional collage structures, implied references to Rauschenberg's combine paintings, sneaker imprints echoing process art, and occasional Pollock-like paint drips all indicate that Baechler is more interested in the ability of images to initiate rich textual layers of semantic play than in an ironic critique of Modernism. Against this rich hybrid background, a generative linkage of measured self-consciousness coalesces, in a manner analogous to the work of dreams.

The artist sends the viewer into a fictive realm vaguely suspended between private memory and the public correspondence of the post card. The signatory of these post cards is an amalgam of discretely aligned identities that may never meet, but at the same time are implicated in a mutual destiny.

Where is the destination of Donald Baechler's painterly post cards? They remain essentially unfinished: destination unknown. Without the cynical escape of irony, the consolation of simple subjectivity, idealism, or utopia, sender and receiver, artist and viewer, are called, by mutual obligation, to write in the possibilities, to assign the address, that is the responsibility of authorship.

MAIA DAMIANOVIC

Profile with Four Palms #1, 1992
Gesso, gouache, collage and coffee on paper
53 x 40½ (134.6 x 102.9 cm)
Collection of the artist;
courtesy of Paul Kasmin Gallery,
New York

40

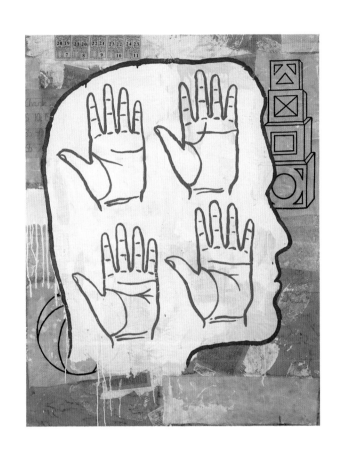

Drew Beattie & Daniel Davidson's collaboration of over four years has focused on issues of identity and individualism. The constantly-evolving formal and conceptual strategies which inform their paint-

B E A T T I E   &   D A V I D S O N

ings are intended to keep both artists and viewers at the edge of what can be understood or accepted as an identifiable human image.

Foremost among Beattie & Davidson's strategies is their use of collaboration. Although this practice is an accepted part of the postmodernist landscape, the contemporary view of painting has generally been that it is, by necessity, a solitary pursuit. For Beattie & Davidson, however, the exigencies of cooperation—having to speak every thought, elaborate every intuition—has helped them to merge their individual efforts into a mutual process of conception and execution.

In early paintings, both artists worked on the same large canvas simultaneously, often without seeing what the other was doing. Continually moving in and out of each other's marks, they were attempting to create the impression of a flow of random mental 'noise'—a field of images in which there was no possibility of distinguishing whose hand (or mind) had made any given part. In each painting, this patina-like accumulation of figure and ground would evolve, like a physical record of time, until both artists agreed that the piece was complete.

A variety of tools are used to blur or veil parts of this image-field from view; these range from rollers and spray bottles to silkscreened echoes of the artist's own drawings. In several canvases, a random scattering of disembodied heads are only seen as ghosts, their inked outlines bleeding through a layer of white paint which has been applied over the entire canvas.

In the *Dozer* paintings, this sense of physical separation from the image is exploited with almost Machiavellian elegance. Giant, cartoony heads are created solely through the manipulation of modified toy trucks and bulldozers on a previously prepared surface. Activated by either radio or voice, these homely mechanical devices lurch around on the wet paint, scraping away a layer of lighter color to reveal a darker ground. The result, a combination of direction, misdirection and accident, is a pattern of marks no hand could ever create.

The ambiguous features—nose? eyes or glasses? moustache, perhaps?—which appear in works like *The Midnight Ride of Paul Revere* and *Call Me Fantastic* suggest themselves as metaphors for the problems of cultural identity facing both artists and viewers. These paintings are as abstract as they are figurative. Neither do their odd titles offer many clues. *Early American Cheaters*, *The Street of Small Cheese*, and *School of Dogs* all suggest a combination of breezy, pop culture vernacular, the overheard phrases of a park bench mumbler, and children's nonsense chants. Like our disintegrating shared identity, Beattie & Davidson's paintings elicit form out of a mutually-invested combination of fantasy and misunderstanding.

MARIA PORGES

The Midnight Ride of Paul Revere, 1993
Oil on canvas
96 x 84
Courtesy of Gallery Paule Anglim, San Francisco

In place of a traditional iconography of the four seasons so lusciously described in eighteenth-century decorative panels, Phyllis Bramson's image collections spring from the artist's consciousness of

PHYLLIS BRAMSON

psychological seasons—of aging, barrenness, and a loss of fertility. These paintings are compartmentalized into fragments of collaged paintings and 1950s-style decorative flourishes that are gorgeously, even obviously kitsch, but despite Bramson's compositional ordering, the basic construction is fantasy: her paintings read like cartouches from a stream-of-consciousness monologue.

Strategies of postmodern pastiche underlie the conceptual constitution of these disjointed assemblages. Bramson borrows freely from production line painters, those decorators who toil in factories in the Philippines to produce clichés—sparkling crystal bowls, dew-dropped roses, gleaming fruit—in repetitive, vacant still lifes. She cuts these shells of paintings into pieces, sands their surfaces to render them less perfect, then blends them skillfully as ornaments for her own invention. In *Broken Cup*, she literally slices through her subject below the eyes, decapitating a figure and amputating a leg to undercut her own earlier representational inclinations.

It is clear that Bramson's cloying clown fragments are threatening and idiosyncratic, less a conventional mask of folly or contemporary surrogate for the white-faced, melancholic, alienated Pierrot, and more like red-nosed signals in a theatrics of unabashed artifice. In *Apple Picker*, the red globes are perverse cartoons that rhyme formally and thematically with the sexual ripeness of fruit. Operating somewhere between full-blown allegory and the seduction of film stills, her compila-

tions of eloquent but disembodied gestures derive their power from the interplay of an either/or situation.

Bramson's notions of abundance are rooted in a 1950s economy: on the other hand, the evident passion of these overwrought tableaux is positively contemporary; her fleshy, feminized palettes and genre detail push us past appreciation and toward visual surfeit. Combining what has been called an "erotics of decoration"[1] with a personal poetics of female aging, Bramson bundles ideas together in the gaps between narrative. In *Suddenly Its Winter*, her borders become floral overindulgences, bands of jewels interspersed among paintings of porcelain figures. It is impossible not to recognize the loss of abundance, the inevitable loss of the bloom in the bosom, that is alluded to by the crystal snowball and the frozen poses of the figurines.

Evoking the exoticism of *Tales of the Arabian Nights*, Bramson tells her stories with powerful subjectivity. Her radiant paintings demonstrate her delight in the very subject matter that she parodies, mimics, and portrays with such conviction. These are bits of stories she tells herself, a mature woman artist who has consistently interrogated the role of fantasy in the construction of identity.

JUDITH RUSSI KIRSHNER

Suddenly Its Winter, 1992
Mixed media and oil on canvas
68 x 68 (172.7 x 172.7 cm)
Courtesy of Brody's Gallery, Washington, D.C. and Phyllis Kind Gallery, Chicago and New York

44

1. Mary D. Sheriff, *Fragonard: Art and Eroticism.* Chicago and London, 1990. 95.

The compelling inner life of Michael Byron's figurative allegories elegantly withdraws narrative structure. Meaning rushes through a labyrinth of possibilities, all related to secrecy and the question

M I C H A E L   B Y R O N

"what happened?" Strange syntaxes and phantasmal image formulations obfuscate any coherent, normative, semantic consumption. Like a haiku, Byron's paintings provide only the bare outline of a story, relying instead on the interaction of highly nuanced and evocative imagistic and linguistic integers set within the envelope of narrative or figurative relations.

A curious semantic resonance typifies his pseudonymous representations. We can only guess the activity or identity (eunuchs? actors?) of the distant, Asian-looking group of figures framed by an expansive, aqueous, backdrop in *When Circumstances Conspire:* the allegory remains indecipherable and strangely mute.

Byron's clotted allegories assume the scatological character of a burst of laughter. His dysfunctional world of pseudo-symbolic whimsy creates distorted vistas without the guarantee of meaning. Despite the realism that is borne out in the postures, attitudes, or gestures of his figures, Byron's paintings cannot compensate for a semantic black hole that is always inherent within figurative representation in particular, and the realistic paradigm in general. Paradoxically, what amounts to figuration's broken promise— its inability to accurately convey emotions or meanings from one person to another— also frees representative painting to engage in unruly semantic play, to assail utopian, romantic, or overly idealistic narrative legacies.

Byron's figures discourage recycling standard narrative identities. An oddity of body postures and sexual implications in

People Sit and Watch (Birth of Performance Art) relates an event that, despite its imagistic record, remains unknowable. The addition of texts that capriciously confuse significant with insignificant messages only further convolutes narrative clarity. The sentence "people sit and watch," floating on the canvas like an awkward label, is conceptually close to what Roland Barthes has designated as the "third meaning."

Byron fuses this semantically opaque possibility, which is always inherent in language, with visual imagery to create a striking, dreamlike quality inviting allusions and seductive innuendos that have more in common with the metaphor of loitering than the phenomenological vigilantism underlying Modernist progressivity or the more conventional precociousness of Surrealist automaticism.

Stripped of comforting symbolic clarity, his figures are closer to the unmediated immediacy of the imaginary, where the body simply exists. Even though creating associations with loss, mourning, and nihilistic regression, Byron's semantic provocations emphasize the fictional construction of how the visually symbolic can begin to redress the established relations of meaning between image and viewer.

MAIA DAMIANOVIC

When Circumstances Conspire, 1991–92,
Oil on panel
117³/₄ x 60¹/₄ (200 x 153 cm)
Collection of the artist

46

Simultaneously creepy and kooky, passionate and calculating, Carole Caroompas's paintings undermine prevailing social mores and alter conceptions of time by sending up the social and sexual stereo-

CAROLE CAROOMPAS

types of classic myths and standard narratives. Her seditious paintings incorporate a multitude of pictorial languages, ranging from anatomical cross sections to clichéd sexual cartoons, to illustrations from social etiquette manuals of the 1950s. Caroompas ladens her charged canvases with contradictory peculiarities, so that each component assumes perverse associations outside the realm of its autonomous idiosyncrasy. Criss-crossing between past and present, classic myths and graphic realities, she constructs blissfully horrific narratives.

In *Before and After Frankenstein: The Woman Who Knew Too Much: Bedside Vigil*, order and ceremony have gone awry in a scene of deliberate licentiousness. Women donning outfits of ancient Greece and others dressed in Shakespearean garb carry the heads of undeniably contemporary men. The women are depicted in shades of green, the heads in black and white, exacerbating their status out of time. Caroompas's women calmly go about their tasks, serving up heads on platters, placing them in a matrimonial bed, or carrying them off to be disposed of in other, unimaginable ways. It is a courtesan coup, revenge for ravages perpetrated upon women by men throughout history. Adding insult to injury, Caroompas has covered the canvas with a checkerboard pattern of red and yellow squares so that, interlocking, they become red crosses—symbols of help and healing. Within each of the yellow squares, a traditionally-coiffed nurse proffers a glass of liquid, presumably some sort of medi-

cine. But served up along with the bodiless heads, it seems at best to be a false antidote.

In her *Spectre and Emanation* series, the war between the sexes is parlayed into poignantly ironic parables. Spectre and Emanation are symbolic figures created by the Romantic poet William Blake to represent the shadow and corporeal forms of desire. In this series of paintings, Caroompas tries to depict this dichotomy and the inevitable frustration which this schism spawns. As in all of her works, men and women are caught up in a frustrating spiral between desire and antagonism, love and hate. Obsession and temptation, as well as discontent and vexation, inform her images; just as passion is often the aggregation of opposite extremes, these paintings seethe with ardent desire. In Caroompas's sapient visions, however, it is a yearning perpetually impeded by the morass of history and the entanglement of deeply ingrained sexual standards.

ALISA TAGER

Before and After Frankenstein: The Woman Who Knew Too Much: Bedside Vigil, 1992
Acrylic on canvas
96 x 108 (243.8 x 274.3 cm)
Courtesy of Sue Spaid Fine Art, Los Angeles

48

Robert Colescott once noted that his purpose as a painter was to interject African Americans (and by extension Latino, Asian, and Native Americans) into art history. To that end he has successfully

R O B E R T   C O L E S C O T T

exploited caricature, satire, irony, and visual punning to subvert familiar visual references, challenging attitudes that have defined hierarchical positions within global politics during the last two thousand years.

Since the mid-1980s, Colescott's compositions have increasingly incorporated multiple figures in several distinct subplots which are often developed in a serial format. These works epitomize the genre of history painting, and Colescott draws on his erudite command of mythological, ethnological, artistic, and literary allusions—the tools that have essentially defined issues of race and gender—to compose compelling narratives.

His recent paintings refine a signature figuration based on a synthesis of the artist's gestural realism of the 1960s, his optical Pop style of the 1970s, and his longstanding appreciation for advertising imagery and cartoons. Works such as *Between Two Worlds* continue explorations of themes of miscegenation, interracial love, and unilateral criteria for beauty that Colescott examined in his *Bathers* series of 1985–86. In *Between Two Worlds*, a distraught mixed-race woman seen in the aura of a mandorla contemplates two women who, flanking her, epitomize the racial pool of her ancestry. Her inclination toward the blonde woman is echoed above, where a black woman (who reminds us of Velasquez's *Venus With a Mirror*) views the image of her wish-fulfilled white self in a mirror. Colescott's figures are almost overtaken by very pronounced 'zones' of color,

which recur in all of his recent paintings. Black auras, flecked with red and white outlines, form the semicircle around the reclining nude in *Between Two Worlds*; figures are similarly isolated by areas of pink or white in *The Atom Bomb in L.A. (Do the Hula-Hula)*.

Colescott's figures also remind us of his artistic compatriots: the pinks, whites, blacks, and reds recall the palette of the late, figurative work of Philip Guston; characters like the longshoreman flexing his muscle at the bottom right of *The Atom Bomb in L.A. (Do the Hula-Hula)* recall the social realism of the 1930s, especially the figuration of Fletcher Martin.[1] But superseding such abundant art-historical references, the individuality of Colescott's various-hued figures denotes the fact that social chemistry invariably defies political interdiction in the realm of human relations.

LOWERY STOKES SIMS

Between Two Worlds, 1992
Acrylic on canvas
84 x 72 (213.4 x 182.9 cm)
Courtesy of Phyllis Kind Gallery,
New York and Chicago

50

1. I would like to acknowledge the participation of Phyllis Kind and Archie Rand in formulating this reading of these paintings, which came out of a spirited discussion at the Phyllis Kind Gallery in January 1993.

Little girls in party dresses fight it out to the finish in Kim Dingle's paintings, but not even the implication of extreme violence brings things to an end in her vivid, unfinished, stop-action images. Embroiled

KIM DINGLE

in pitched battles or locked in ambivalent embraces, Dingle's heroines struggle to recover from the mayhem and antagonism that surrounds them; they both resist and intensify the childish fantasy of setting things right once and for all. These naughty and vulnerable infants and kids thus dramatize some of the contradictory impulses at the root of racism. Dingle's stripped-down pictures of dressed-up girls trace divisions between peoples to divisions within individuals—to the complex, psychological territory where desire and denial collide and fear and fantasy conspire to create impressions that may not be true but are truly difficult to defy.

A pair of her paintings contends that no relationship between the races is defined by clear-cut oppositions. Structurally, *Black Girl Dragging White Girl* and *White Girl Trying to Lift Black Girl* appear to be complementary elements that add up to a harmonious whole. Imagistically, however, they do not account for meaning by dividing the world into simple, dualistic categories. In Dingle's larger-than-life-size works, meaning resides in the details. *Black Girl Dragging White Girl* shows a determined black girl straining to lift a similarly dressed white girl who looks as if she's knocked-out, sound asleep, or seriously ill. If the black girl's inner strength is incommensurate with her physical ability, the white girl's consciousness is separated even further from her surroundings: completely oblivious, she is a weighty burden in a narrative whose resolution we cannot know. In *White Girl Trying to Lift Black Girl*, while both kids are alert, they are likewise caught up in an indeterminate story. Again, the black girl's face is the more expressive: she seems extremely uneasy in the grip of her playmate, as if holiday games have gone too far, turning fun into an eerily adult power struggle, in which anger builds and rage is barely contained. Real and imagined helplessness, control masked as assistance, genuine compassion, and selfless risk take concrete shape in Dingle's potent diptych. As each viewer is drawn into these pictures, personal associations and intimate memories flesh out narratives that are as compelling as they are ambiguous and open-ended.

Dingle's images of lifter and lifted reveal that the structuralist dream—a morally equivalent universe where every subject can be plugged into and substituted among various positions—is an abstract fantasy unsuited for the complexities of the real world. Her doubled study of otherness compels us to see that the mismatches between categories and the selves who are meant to fill them constitute the charged ground on which individual identity and cultural difference are played out. By accentuating these differences, her art creates the possibility that our habitual projections might get turned around, leading us toward introspection and potentially toward self-transformation.

DAVID PAGEL

Black Girl Dragging White Girl, 1992
Oil and charcoal on linen
72 x 60 (182.9 x 152.4 cm)
Collection Corcoran Gallery of Art
Gift of the Women's Committee

52

Poised on the precipice between fantasy and reality, daydream and delusion, Inga Frick's paintings are manic forays into the subconscious. Figures float through her chaotic melanges of illusionary objects

I N G A   F R I C K

and abstractions in a mellifluous flurry of shapes and colors; images move in and out of focus and back and forth through disjointed narratives. Assemblies of dissonant juxtapositions, Frick's paintings are more hallucinatory than aggressive, occupying that strangely atemporal realm of dreams where giant bananas truly can float above a naked geisha doing the wash.

Indeed, this type of occurrence is common in Frick's out-of-whack world. In *Black and White and Read All Over*, birds' nests, naked body parts, and fairytale fragments push cognition through a finely meshed sieve. Everything is familiar, yet nothing can be understood: this is reinforced by the artist's decision to forego canvas or linen for a patterned fabric whose illustrations of fairytales deepens the painting's surface cacophony. Designed to be hung in a corner, the painting reads like an open book, an effect echoed by the centrally located outline of a figure reading. Frick has drawn the figure from the viewer's perspective, so that viewing it is like looking down at one's own body; it is as if the viewer is the reader, entering into the text through the positions of this amorphous, unidentified character. Bordering the painting's left edge, a narrow black-and-white checkered panel with black text superimposed on it abruptly halts such hazy visions. But the pattern also makes it impossible to discern the text, in effect making these written words just as mysterious and ungraspable as the artist's visual narrative. Frick has created a story within a story within a story, the

pictorial equivalent of standing between two mirrors and watching your reflection extend into infinity.

In *Shadow Box*, a lone bicyclist, again painted from the viewer's perspective, pedals across an unfamiliar galaxy while clutching a purple Popsicle. Faint outlines of dancing couples in old-fashioned apparel form ethereal constellations in a bizarre star system. An airbrushed man in a tuxedo hovers upside down from the painting's topside, while the legs of his incompletely rendered dance partner kick out to one side. It's an intergalactic waltz or jitterbug through which Frick's decidedly contemporary cyclist nonchalantly pedals. In her collusion of times, places and spaces, Frick pushes narrative resolution and recognizable information into an abyss of extravagant imagination: entering *Shadow Box* is like stepping through the looking glass, like Alice, we enter into an unknown place of perverse whimsies. Subverting expectation and undermining concise interpretations, Frick consistently pushes and twists the boundaries of perception. Her paintings are ecstatic fabrications of an absurdly poetic fervor. Fancifully mysterious, her rhapsodic flights venture into quixotic realms that suggest the possibilities inherent to the quintessence of humanity.

ALISA TAGER

Shadow Box, 1992
Acrylic and pencil on fabric
76¾ x 96 (194.9 x 243.8 cm)
Courtesy of Jones Troyer
Fitzpatrick Gallery,
Washington, D.C.

54

Unadulterated innocence collides with apocalyptic violence in Charles Garabedian's comic classicism. At once epic, endearing, and bloody, his series *Study for the Iliad* gives fleshy substance

CHARLES GARABEDIAN

to the fact that life meets us head-on. Despite our desire to be prepared for the future, Garabedian seems to be saying, fate never allows us rehearsals or trial runs, but often catches us at our most hapless and helpless—in impossible dramas and difficult predicaments, in situations that we are rarely ready to accept and absolutely powerless to undo.

Nearly all of the pictures in Garabedian's series depict a single, fleeting moment of human consciousness: one that occurs immediately after damage has been done and just before consciousness of that damage occurs. The lumpy, contorted figures in his lyrical paintings of tragic events awkwardly inhabit this thin slice of time. As if timelessly suspended in a strange, dreamlike state, their solid bodies and implied consciousnesses are governed neither by the pure physicality of animal activity nor the complex reflections of self-critical recollection.

Some of Garabedian's heroes seem to be unconscious, gravely wounded, even dead. Others appear to be blissfully asleep, lost in mindless reverie, or in shock. The most intriguing look curious and inquisitive despite having been pierced by long spears, having lost limbs, or having even been decapitated. A headless nude, who recurs in several paintings, sits casually on the ground, holding his hand in front of the space where his face would be if his head weren't missing. A stream of blood spurts into his hand, as if to confirm what he's suspected, even though trauma and horror have not yet registered.

Garabedian's uncanny paintings are perversely sweet; they aren't macabre descriptions of the gory details of untimely deaths so much as existentialist accounts of how we process bodily phenomena, making sense of sensations, usually too late to make much difference in the immediacy of the present. What takes shape in his art is a strange moment that seems to exist outside of time—not in the sense that it belongs to a transcendental realm of eternal perfection, but in the sense that it is profoundly unknown or alien, not yet apprehended by rationality or brought into the continuum of history.

Garabedian's thoroughly contemporary rendition of the ancient poem ascribed to Homer travels back in time to take us somewhere else. Never nostalgic, sentimental, or opportunistic, his series employs a founding monument of Western culture to emphasize the vitality of the moment. Far from attempting to extend a daunting lineage of supposedly static masterpieces, his *Study for the Iliad* demonstrates that creativity, like a suddenly opened wound, springs from any ungoverned moment—when sensations and interpretations are temporarily out of control and up for grabs.

DAVID PAGEL

Study for the Iliad, 1992
Acrylic on panel
48 x 60 (121.9 x 152.4 cm)
Courtesy of the artist,
L.A. Louver, Inc., Venice, California,
and Gallery Paule Anglim,
San Francisco

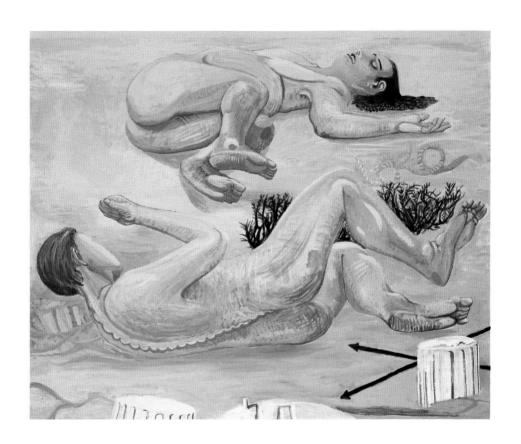

57

A tragedy, then, is the imitation of an action that is serious, complete in itself, and has a certain magnitude. It arouses pity and fear wherewith to accomplish a catharsis of such emotions.

—Aristotle

L E O N   G O L U B

The demonic is anxiety about the good. In innocence, freedom was not posited as freedom: possibility was anxiety in the individual. In the demonic, the relation is reversed. Freedom is posited as unfreedom, because freedom is lost. Here again freedom's possibility is anxiety. The difference is absolute, because freedom's possibility appears here in relation to unfreedom, which is the very opposite of innocence, which is a qualification disposed toward freedom.

—Kierkegaard

Leon Golub could be described as the painter of the *inhuman* condition. His work deals with what Karl Jaspers has called "anonymous powers." These anonymous powers are the ancient demons of our religiously deprived modern world—the demons of nothingness. In Golub's paintings, being and nothingness struggle with each other for existence.

Recently, as in *So Much the Worse*, Leon Golub has added graffiti to his repertory of images. Rudely scratched statements and drawings are literally worked into the skin of the paintings like tattoos. Here the letter becomes again the calligraphy of the nonrepresentable, or, in existential terms, *nothingness*.

Graffiti looks back to the origin of the nonrepresentable. The nonrepresentable had its beginnings in the *cave*, which contained the secrets of birth and death. Secrets that only the *women* knew. For the men who were excluded from the events in the cave—childbearing, the spiral dance, the graffiti on its walls—

the cave became the nonrepresentable, the *Other*.

It is the same cave that with Plato, in a process of inversion, became the birthplace of (male) philosophy—a philosophy whose only concern is the segregation from the nonrepresentable. Its truth had to originate therefore in the *light* (the enlightenment)—as opposed to the darkness of the cave. The cave itself became the mysterious and terrifying *labyrinth*. The archaic gesture of graffiti, once itself the signified, became the signifier or the *letter*.

Golub's paintings attain an existentialist form of catharsis which replaces the Aristotelian fear with a Kierkegaardian anxiety—an anxiety that is begotten by nothingness. When it seems that the inhuman has gotten the better of us, his paintings accomplish this catharsis by taking all the terrors committed by the modern world upon themselves, and, in an act of momentary redemption, returning us to a state of innocence, giving pause to remember our humanity.

KLAUS OTTMANN

Jubilance, 1993
Acrylic on linen
76 x 121 (193 x 307.3 cm)
Courtesy of the artist and
Josh Baer Gallery, New York

In 1883 John Singer Sargent wrote to a friend about his desire to paint the wife of a Parisian Banker, Virginie Gautreau, who grew up, like many young upper-class women of the time, to be a 'profes-

C A T H E R I N E　　H O W E

sional beauty' assigned to serve as an ornamental element at balls and dinners. "I have a great desire to paint her portrait and have reason to think she would allow it and is waiting for someone to propose this homage to her beauty. If you are '*bien avec elle*' and will see her in Paris you might tell her that I am a man of *prodigious talent*."

Her portrait, which later became known as *Madame X*, when first shown created a traumatic impression on the public that matched the scandal over Manet's *Olympia*. It presented an unusually self-assured woman of considerable beauty with extremely pale skin posing in a long, black dress.

What makes this portrait so remarkable is the fact that the desire of the painter was taken over by the desire of the model. In his attempt to transform her body into an abstract object of beauty, Sargent exposed it as the subject of its own desire rather than that of the (male) artist.

In Catherine Howe's paintings, rendered with the gestural virtuosity of Abstract Expressionism, Willem de Kooning's brushstrokes and Clyfford Still's patches of color form the backdrops for her luscious portraits of white and black women of great confidence and poise.

Portraits of white women, whose features are adapted from various paintings by Sargent, stand in front of de Kooning-style backgrounds, displaying a triumphant spirit. A backdrop reminiscent of Still gives Howe's portraits of black women, who have no specific art-historical origin, a more ambiguous, somber quality.

In Howe's *Pink Arabesque*, de Kooning's loose brushstrokes are transformed into ornamental swags and streamers that evoke the joyous turn-of-the-century ballrooms of Boston and Atlanta; in *Mirage*, Still's serene, orange color field is suggestive of the sun-filled cornfields of the American Midwest or South.

There is a curious reversal at work in these paintings: the male heroic gesture of Abstract Expressionism, which relegated women to a subordinate role, is reduced to a decorative backdrop.

Howe's paintings, however, go beyond mere mimicry or a feminist comment on the notorious sexism and gynephobia of Abstract Expressionism. They are about both the absence and presence of women in painting. To accomplish this, they stage a reversed masquerade: the woman's desire situates the masculine, not vice-versa. Howe deliberately makes the masculine assume a decorative style and posture traditionally assigned to women. She picks up where Sargent left off, letting her heroines experience their own desire rather than that of the painter.

KLAUS OTTMANN

60

Mirage, 1993
Oil on linen
84 x 60 (213.4 x 152.4 cm)
Collection Alan P. Power,
Venice, California

Of the two questions we asked, 'Why are we unable to laugh at a joke we have made ourselves?' and 'Why are we driven to tell our own joke to someone else?', the first has so far evaded our reply. We can only suspect

D A V I D   H U M P H R E Y

that there is an intimate connection between the two facts that have to be explained: that we are compelled to tell our joke to someone else because we are unable to laugh at it.

—Freud

When one looks at David Humphrey's paintings, it is almost impossible not to be reminded of Freud's writings on the subject of jokes. Like jokes, his paintings originate in a highly personal place but require the participation of a third person to work. In *Jokes and Their Relation to the Unconscious*, Freud argues that the formation of jokes is intimately related to the "dream-work" discussed in his *Interpretation of Dreams*. Dream-work and joke-work converge in the methods of condensation (the compression of content into common elements), displacement (the shifting of minor, marginal matters to positions of central importance), and indirect representation (the representation by allusion or analogy) but differ fundamentally in their social behavior: "A dream is a completely asocial mental product . . . . The joke, on the other hand, is the most social of all mental functions that aim at a yield of pleasure . . . . Its completion requires the participation of someone else in the mental process it starts . . . . A dream still remains a wish, even though one that has been made unrecognizable; a joke is developed play . . . . Dreams serve predominantly for the avoidance of unpleasure, jokes for the attainment of pleasure."

Using the photographic mementos of his family—which are photocopied and scanned, then manipulated on a computer screen before being painted onto the canvas—Humphrey provides an emotional distance for himself while bringing a familiar, even familial, nearness to the beholder.

Humphrey's low-resolution, blown-up images are joined by biomorphic shapes, paint drips, and cartoony thought bubbles, which add a surrealist wit to the intimate subject matter of the work. In *Guest* the head of a young woman, which appears as a shifted double image, is adorned with a headband of paint drips and a painted lock of hair—the latter a common element in Humphrey's paintings, attesting to his preoccupation with hair as a signifying fetish. In *Your Sponge*, a large thought bubble/paint drip contains a blowup from a second photograph, which spills over the primary image like a 1960s B-movie representation of Freud's unconscious.

As Freud said in regard to the joke, each painting is a "double-dealing rascal who serves two masters at once." No longer the artist's memories alone, Humphrey's family fictions become ours as well.

KLAUS OTTMANN

62

Your Sponge, 1992
Oil on canvas
82 x 72 (208.3 x 182.9 cm)
Courtesy of McKee Gallery,
New York

In Hung Liu's work, images from China's past act as metaphors for the anomie of cultural disintegration and loss of context that has become a constant experience in this century. Liu, who came of age in

H U N G   L I U

China during the Cultural Revolution, was trained there as a Social Realist. Since the mid-1980s, she has lived and worked in the United States, using her traditional academic training to create a body of work which examines problems of cultural and sexual identity through the lens of postmodern practice.

Since 1988, Liu has painted mainly from historical photographs depicting Chinese prostitutes from around the turn of the century. These women are pictured in and among props, costumes, and scenery that would have been quite strange to Asian eyes at the time. Presumably, the motive for posing these women with telephones, cars, or Victorian furniture was to make them more attractive and/or exotic to potential customers. Liu's appropriations of these photographs, however, are not so much a homily on the oppression and commodification of these women as they are a commentary on the discordant fictions which are created when two cultures collide.

In *Raft of the Medusa*, Liu ironically revises Géricault's famous heroic composition. Obsessed with authenticity, the French painter strove to make his enormous canvas of half-naked men clinging to a raft as grippingly realistic as possible, despite the fact that his vision was constructed piecemeal out of contradictory survivor's accounts and the artist's own highly fertile imagination. In contrast, the scene Liu depicts is almost aggressively artificial. What appears to be a boy and girl sitting quietly in a little boat is, in fact, a double-exposed studio portrait of the same young woman, dressed appropriately to convey the erotic values of either gender. By basing her *Medusa* on a photograph of a real person, Liu reminds us that, unlike Géricault's rafters, this unsmiling young prostitute could only survive as a projection of the viewer's imaginative desires.

In *Swan Song*, Liu eschews unified pictorial space completely. Two separate fields of black and white serve as the background for the printed words and music of a Revolutionary hymn titled "A Proletarian Fights All His Life for the People's Revolution." This text, in turn, serves as the frame for literally decontextualized images of dancers from the Red Detachment. Here, Liu resolves the relationship between figure and ground by simply removing the latter entirely, emphasizing both the flatness and iconic quality of these leaping young women. Above them, in several places, monochrome vignettes of women's hands and faces are superimposed over the stirring phrases of the song. These fragmented views suggest something seen from far away, reminding us that all of the different pasts represented by these women are equally remote. In Liu's hands, this proletarian dirge becomes the swan song not only for the powerless prostitute or the woman with bound feet, but for the prancing Cultural Revolutionaries as well.

MARIA PORGES

Raft of the Medusa, 1992
Oil on canvas with lacquered wood and mixed media
61 x 96 x 8½
(154.9 x 243.8 x 21.6 cm)
Collection Eric and Barbara Dobkin

Painterliness is often the mark of instinctive expression, and the pathos, partial successes, and inevitable failures of the creative process are readily evident in Jim Lutes's cursive gestures. Lutes swirls

J I M   L U T E S

his pigments into a tangle of brushstrokes, some delicately linear, others fat and tubular. His revelations of psychic and physical vulnerability appear unflattering, even embarrassing, and yet authentic. This is underscored by titles like *Street Sucker, Hero no More, Skidder, Sinker,* and *Loaf of Woe*. Paintings become head-shaped walls: in-our-face, confrontational puns that undermine good taste, as Lutes's exquisite handling of crude subject matter seduces us with powerful contradictions.

Where Lutes's earlier paintings told surreal dreams of grotesque, swollen body parts inhabiting grimy, littered, urban nightmares, painterliness now constitutes his primary content. A darker side is always visible in his apparently senseless, melancholic scatters; in these works, paradoxes of chaos stubbornly refuse to disappear. These are allegories of deformity; they resist transfiguration but are tied into a profile shape by a bright thread, a lasso that only hints at bodily integrity.

In *Pacified Night*, we witness Lutes's grim humor. Although the small child in an alley suggests the nostalgia of biographical recollection, these images—dreamt and painted "by a guy who has heard gunshots at night"—emerge from the artist's perception of urban reality. Bits of perspective, suggested by architectural planes, define a bed and a room, yet recognizable details swim in and out of focus, dissolving like phantoms of recognition, people we forgot we met, or dreams we hope to forget. In a reversal of the historical relationship between abstraction and figuration, where flesh and paint are formally synonymous, these images never quite unravel. Instead, they always court disintegration. They slide away then reassemble as organic riots of confetti, flames, and teeth.

Lute appreciates the timeless richness of masters such as Brueghel and Rubens, but at the same time he depends on his resistance to figurative impulses; his paintings neither repudiate nor invest in such heroic conventions. Rather, his work moves freely, layering oppositional concepts such as literal and abstract, visible and invisible. Signs of the artist's ongoing aesthetic negotiation, which suggests painting as speculation, shimmer like punctuation marks across his piles of swarming strokes. Reinforcing this, the palette Lutes chooses is thoroughly post-modern, the colors sour to day-glo shrill, and the sensibility manic. Images threaten to dissolve into paint, then cohere into a head defined by clues like lips or a flattop bristle haircut. No longer tied to the representation of visceral and genital organs, ribbons of color in *Too Lips* coalesce into a hallucinatory head, flayed save an unmoored, protruding smile and a string of tiny eyes arranged Rockette-style along the side. In this work, as in all of Lutes's paintings, the skin of the painting—fleshy, crusted, scabby—is peeled back to represent a vision which, more often than not, is a face or mask for the artist.

JUDITH RUSSI KIRSHNER

Too Lips, 1992
Oil on linen
60 x 42 (152.4 x 106.7 cm)
Collection Arthur G. Rosen,
New York

Eternal youth is not as ideal as it would seem in Kerry James Marshall's arresting portraits of black teenagers. Although the boys and girls who inhabit his paintings will never grow old, they have also lost

KERRY JAMES MARSHALL

their chance to be children. The price they have unwillingly paid for freedom from adulthood's responsibilities is death.

Titled *The Lost Boys*, Marshall's powerful pictures of fictitious kids memorialize the anonymous, innocent children we usually know only through newspaper stories, when their lives are suddenly cut short by senseless, random violence. His stylized, life-size portraits also acknowledge a generation's increasing incapacity to play—to abandon oneself to the joy of purposeless amusement and the thrill of carefree recreation, among the security of friends and the familiarity of neighborhood.

The intense, often somber, dignified faces in Marshall's stirring images convey sentiments well beyond their years, as if his youthful, nicknamed sitters (AKA Li'l Bit, AKA Baby Brother) are prematurely wise to the cruelty of fate and the blindness of society. Their adult demeanor, however, is not built upon rich, personal histories or accumulated childhood experiences, but instead stands in as a troubling, inadequate substitute for gradual maturation, protected exploration, and drawn-out discovery. Marshall's series pays equal homage to victims of violence and those who live through it, in a world so dangerous that just being a kid is becoming a more unattainable luxury or impossible fantasy than any ordinary expectation.

In an 8 x 10 foot painting from the same series, two boys play with toys as if they don't really know what they're supposed to be doing: they seem to be stiffly

rehearsing roles they don't wholly understand. One clutches a pink plastic water pistol and strikes a pose that wants to be tough, even threatening, but is more tentative and sad. The other grips the wheel of a play racecar and stares out at the viewer, as if for approval or instruction, but also somewhat defiantly, as if to say, with his eyes, that it's no fault of his that he feels out of place among playthings.

Other elements intensify the connection between frivolous fun and deadly seriousness. A police line wraps, like a serpent, around a tree of life that bears bullets instead of fruit. A pair of pearly gates frames the scene, and a foregrounded kewpie doll, commonly placed on the graves of rural black children, adds to a sense of suspended otherworldliness. The word "Power," written in bright yellow capitals on the base of the racecar ride, appears crowded between the pink gun and orange doll, subtly insisting that in fun and games lies a serious source of future strength. Marshall's art twice makes a place for the pleasure of recreation: as a memorial for the children to whom play (and life) is denied, and for his viewers, to whom his potent, politically engaged paintings never preach, but always provide a small free space in which meaning can echo and resonate.

DAVID PAGEL

The Lost Boys, 1993
Acrylic on canvas
104 x 120 (264.2 x 304.8 cm)
Courtesy of the Principal
Financial Group and
Koplin Gallery, Los Angeles

Since the late 1970s Melissa Miller has chosen animals as the subjects of her powerful, enigmatic narrative dramas. Expressionistically painted, often in bright colors, her work owes a debt to tradi-

M E L I S S A   M I L L E R

tional 'animal' painters such as Sir Edwin Landseer, as well as eighteenth-century Japanese prints, the folk tales of New Mexico and the Southwest, and her own rural childhood in Southern Texas. In her paintings of tigers, bears, and leopards from the early 1980s, the boundaries of nature are often dissolved—humans and animals behave in similar ways, reflecting Miller's deeply held belief in the interdependence of all life forms.

In 1986, Miller began a series of paintings of spirits, demons, and angels in which animals confront images of their own ghosts or the skeletons of other creatures; this series culminates in *Decision* and *The Temptation of Saint Anthony. Decision* represents Miller's personal interpretation of issues of appearance and reality, truth and deception, and the ability of all creatures, including humans, to change their identities. By contrast, Miller became interested in the story of Saint Anthony through her extensive study of art history; images of the ascetic saint beset by demons as he struggled in the wilderness—a common artistic theme since the Renaissance—corresponded with her own visual explorations of ghost and demon imagery. This general visual interest in the imagery developed into a more intense study of the story of the life of the saint, specifically Flaubert's 1874 version, which she found "packed with images" that echoed her desire to depict inner, psychological states.[1]

Earlier works in this series are populated with fantastic, imagined creatures, but only one form in *Temptation of Saint Anthony*—the four-headed dog—can be said to be truly invented. Ultimately, Miller believes that the most frightening things are those familiar images that have undergone a slight metamorphosis. Here, she chose an elk charging and struggling with a blazing ball of fire to personify the saint's struggle, and she comprised her fire demon of a host of traditional but ambiguous Christian symbols—angel, snake, dog—as well as more subtle images, such as the rose, symbol of transient beauty and the illusion of good.

Miller was drawn to the story of Saint Anthony because of the "excruciating self-scrutiny" of the saint as he battled not only the obvious human vices of greed, envy, sloth, and vanity, but also as he addressed the more subtle questions of life—the extremity of his withdrawal into the wilderness in pursuit of God, for example, or the questionable wisdom of the haste with which he made his decision. In these recent works, her most complex to date in both composition and content, Melissa Miller portrays a powerful inner reality, informing her vast art-historical knowledge with a late twentieth-century understanding of the human psyche.

MARLA PRICE

The Temptation of Saint Anthony, 1993
Oil on linen
51 x 76 (129.5 x 193 cm)
The Barrett Collection,
Dallas

70

1. Interview with the artist, June 3, 1993.

Vicious, demented, yet wickedly funny, Manuel Ocampo's monstrous paintings take you to hell in a handbasket. On the one-way trip, you come face-to-face with hooded, gun-wielding fiends, tribesmen

M A N U E L   O C A M P O

hacking captives to bits, and sleepy-eyed mutants ripping the flesh of their sex partners. In the gruesome world depicted by the Philippine-born, Los Angeles-based artist, such mythic clichés take on a ferocious life of their own. Like anonymous, out-of-control Frankensteins, they fail to function as we want them to: their extremity traps us in the ugliness of our ignorance. Rather than reinforcing racist prejudices—or putting some psychological distance between 'us' and 'them'—Ocampo's catastrophic dramas warp stereotypes so relentlessly that no one escapes deformation.

Loaded symbols—such as Nazi swastikas and Christian crosses—share the stage with hooded Ku Klux Klansmen, decapitated men, winged beasts, and swollen globes that stand in as various body parts of mix-and-match caricatures. Fragmented messages in English, French, Hebrew, Sanskrit, Spanish, and Tagalog (an indigenous Philippine language) adorn otherwise unrelated scenarios. Quotes from famous Communists and comical Dadaists, notorious Fascists and benevolent Christians, forgotten alchemists and grim existentialists, nineteenth-century liberals and twentieth-century xenophobes all contribute to Ocampo's overheated cacophony of rampant hybridization. Like unwanted bastards or unidentifiable mongrels, his degenerate yet quite traditional paintings force civilization's highest aspirations into an unholy alliance with its rude underbelly, making perverse, nightmarish sense.

Once Again First in the World ridicules the notion of cultural purity and the hypocrisy of originary claims. By casting the avant garde's valorization of originality in terms of quasi-fascistic attempts to purge otherness and impurity, Ocampo's heraldic image mocks Modernism's ideal of an art free of politics. Titled after a sarcastic statement made by John Heartfield, Dadaist collagist and member of the German resistance to Hitler, this painting suggests that beginning anew is a deluded fantasy shared mainly by academics, out-of-touch artists, and manipulative politicians.

One of the ironies of his art is the relationship between his artistic training and his current work. Ocampo learned his trademark technical virtuosity not from Modernist mentors, but from religious instructors who illustrated the Catholic canon for the Philippino faithful. Thus armed, he illuminates the bad dream of multiculturalism. In his pictures, Western culture's newest dogma is not an ideal dream in which 'difference' is fostered and respected, but a pathetic epiphenomenon of international commerce and multinational capital. Ocampo refuses to play the game of equating powerlessness with goodness, domination with evil, in order to ensure the popularity of his work. In his tormented maelstroms of politics and culture, although art is swallowed up by propaganda, it paradoxically takes on more power when it addresses all sides of our contradictory, impure, and embattled world.

DAVID PAGEL

Once Again First in the World, 1993
Oil on linen
96 x 96 (243.8 x 243.8 cm)
Collection Jean Pigozzi, Geneva;
Courtesy Fred Hoffman Fine Art,
Los Angeles

72

Unlike the coolly opaque work of most image-text artists, Deborah Oropallo's highly handcrafted, deliberately theatrical paintings seem to invite the viewer to step into another time. Like well-trained

D E B O R A H   O R O P A L L O

actors, spotlit words and figures float across the stage: unset jewels in a mellow, varnished gloom, hinting at fascinating *noir* narratives. The intention of these canvases, however, is not to invoke mere nostalgia or sentiment. For Oropallo, the old-fashioned conventions of realist painting have become a vehicle for the expression of disturbingly contemporary feelings and ideas.

The seemingly disparate source materials she draws upon for these images range from instruction manuals for the practice of magic, first aid, and games, to fairytales, folk myths, and alphabet rhymes. What these texts have in common is the construction of a world in which events and their consequences are clearly (and, sometimes, ominously) linked—although the usual happily-ever-after outcome is often short-circuited by the artist's adroit manipulation of the story's elements.

Not unlike a magician, Oropallo uses a number of theatrical strategies and devices to accomplish her goal. Figures, objects, and the old-fashioned lettering in these works are often blurred, their dissolving forms implying both a loss of meaning, as if leached out over time, and a distance so great that the certainty of sharp focus is no longer possible. In *The Wolf*, the image of Little Red Riding Hood and her lupine companion seem to melt into the chiaroscuro, while painted 'echoes' of their figures suggest that, in search of the perfect point of view, it is actually necessary for the viewer to adopt a shifting perspective.

This faintly vertiginous feeling of restless movement is further emphasized by the field of closely-spaced bars which surrounds the tiny forest clearing. Like a scrim, these stripes create a visual layer through which image and text can only be seen with difficulty, creating allusions to problems of perception as well as comprehension.

Over and over, Oropallo denies us the certainty or closure that myths or fairy tales traditionally provide. The oval of a shooting target superimposed over the wolf's false, doggy smile implies that Little Red's problems could be solved before they happen by a sniper's bullet (although, by the location of the target, the implied gunman is standing somewhere behind us, pointing a rifle at our backs). As appealing as this radical revision seems, many of Oropallo's other paintings of this story suggest an ambivalence toward the consequences of such censorious textual interventions. Her job, it seems, is to leave us with more questions than answers: suggesting, perhaps, that we should not rely on faith alone, but use our wits as well. Even the innocent alphabet rhyme bannered across the background of *Woodsman*—"*A* is for axe and that we all know; *B* is for boy who can use it also"—takes on a different meaning when we notice that the empty-handed axeman whose recumbent form repeats across the canvas could as easily be dead as fast asleep.

MARIA PORGES

74

The Wolf, 1993
Oil on canvas
86 x 64 (218.4 x 162.6 cm)
Collection of
Anne MacDonald,
Tiburon, California

Unlike the literal eschatology currently prevalent in much political art, Elena Sisto's multifaceted paintings, spanning a nexus of pictorial possibilities and languages, sidestep overtly feminist subjec-

E L E N A   S I S T O

tivity. By remaining sufficiently close to conventional representation, her obsessive elaborations of the female figure act out in subversive complicity an imagistic refiguration more complicated than any simple ideological affirmation or denial.

Sisto's scenario is one of stolen identities. In *What Would I Do Without You?*, bimbos, those stereotypically stupid female figures from American cartoon culture, appear clad in a polka dot bikini, as a voluptuous pin-up girl, and as a distracted blond posed against a vaguely Modernist painterly abstraction that evokes the canvases of Arshile Gorky, Willem de Kooning, or the artists of the School of Paris. However, unlike the expansive, gestural bravura inherent to Abstract Expressionism, Sisto's smaller canvases conjure up a more reflective intimacy. Her reconstructed bimbo becomes a corrosive sign, an image as a contagion of interlocked effects, where different notions of beauty, sensuality, repulsion, and attraction simultaneously wrestle, as if a desire unleashed.

By incessantly juxtaposing female stereotypes with various art-historical references—from the Twombly-esque background in *Look For Me*, to the classical, Matisse-like arabesques in *Like The Mirror,* or the luxurious luminescent skin, reminiscent of Ingres' Odalisques—Sisto eccentrically elaborates, aggravates, or irreverently tampers with representation, often to the point where the caricatured voluptuousness of the curves of her figures coalesce into abstraction. These elaborations work as representational infelicities:

conscious misinterpretations of conventional representations that refer, in this new context, to a distorted intertextual figuration that detours our predilection for a consumerist display replete with predictable sexual commodity status.

In *Eve*, Sisto treats the painting as though it were an actual body, as if the physically absorbing lushness of the figure's skin, an essentially feminine attribute, would effect an immediate sensuality with the visual ability to overpower any negative symbolic connotations conjured by the adjacent serpentine form. Such visual emphasis daringly blurs conventional dialectical clarity, and an almost erotic entanglement ensues.

Elaborated by Sisto, the figure of the bimbo is no longer the body upon which culture has imposed a certain insidious representation of women or writing of history. Instead, it embodies originary imagery, discovering itself through whirls of color and form, as the lines of the body unfold unarrested. Sisto's figuration is in flux with all the differential effects of identity. In stark contrast to the often indifferent and even incidental culture bank of feminine images, from the physical reality of Chinese footbinding to the Hollywood concoction of Betty Boop, each of Sisto's bimbo paintings ask to be read thoughtfully and specifically, as a progression toward a mercurial *jouissance* that exhorts the autonomy of the body.

MAIA DAMIANOVIC

76

What Would I Do Without You?, 1992
Tempera on linen
18¼ x 42 (46.4 x 106.7 cm)
Courtesy of Germans Van Eck
Gallery, New York

When you enter the portals of the Temple of Dendur at the Metropolitan Museum of Art, you gradually become aware of the extensive graffiti that has been carved into the wall surfaces. These mementos

N A N C Y   S P E R O

of visitors, accumulated over many centuries, impact the temple's original relief carvings: in effect, they confuse our perception of time and place.

In *Sacred and Profane Love*, Nancy Spero presents specters from other times on lengths of paper scrolled across the walls of contemporary galleries. Positioned at molding height, this work affirms its relationship to antiquity's insistence that narrative should have an architectural function. Spero's stamped and printed images, which often recur in her work, have been culled from existing images from Crete, Greece, Phoenicia, Egypt, and other pre-Christian sites. In *Sacred and Profane Love*, we see the nude female reveler cavorting with fake phalli, the winged gorgon with her curlicue coiffure and grimacing countenance, and the forgotten Celtic goddess Sheela-na-gig, who exposes her vulva.

Spero's women do not exhibit ladylike behavior. They prance about, their breasts proudly thrust outward, or pose, often in the nude, sticking out their tongues or exposing their genitals: they are thoroughly unfettered by fashion or social mores. This transgressive posturing symbolizes the reclamation of a self-determined female expression that began to occupy Spero in the early 1970s, when she abandoned easel painting for the immediacy of collaged graphic and typographical elements. Spero calculated the arrangement of text and the accompanying figures so that mass and void alternated like the rising and falling sounds and respites of musical scores or spoken

scripts. Since the early 1980s she has moved away from texts, which often bound her images to the thoughts of others: instead, the artist overlaps various gestures, postures, and poses that she draws from her bank of over 270 figural types. Arrayed on the wall like a frieze, they communicate on their own, like hieroglyphs.[1] In different contexts, their symbolic resonance might change, but in all these works Spero invariably speaks to the condition of women today, all over the world.

Along with the older images, she also draws on contemporary sources, such as the strange slug-headed figure in *Sacred and Profane Love*, which Spero discovered in a painting by a woman beset with insanity. In another case the Semitic goddess Lilith, surrounded by animals that pay homage to her essential femaleness, accompanies a mirrored imprint of a cross-dressing woman, based on a photograph taken in the 1920s, that once again reaffirms the potency and potentiality of assertive femininity.

LOWERY STOKES SIMS

Sacred and Profane Love, (details) 1993
Handprinting and printed collage on paper
20½ x 888 (52.1 x 2,255.5 cm)
Courtesy of the artist and Josh Baer Gallery, New York

1. Conversation with the artist, May 1993.

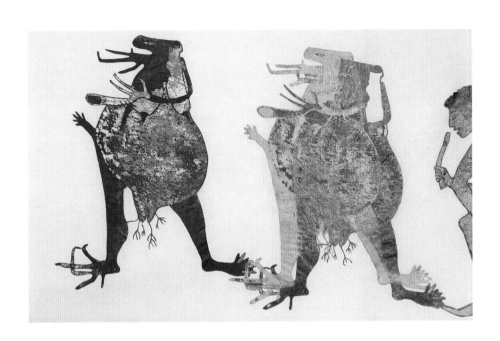

Exhibitions are listed in chronological order. An asterisk (*) denotes a one-person exhibition.

B I O G R A P H I E S

IDA APPLEBROOG

Born 1929, Bronx, New York
Lives New York City

Education

1950   Institute of Applied Arts and Sciences, New York
1968   School of the Art Institute of Chicago

Fellowships and Awards

1990   Guggenheim Fellowship
1991–1992   Milton Avery Professorship, Bard College, New York

Selected Exhibitions

1970   *South 8*, Fine Arts Museum, San Diego.
1971   *Soft Forms: Ida Horowitz*, Palomar College, San Marcos, California.
1972   *Invisible/Visible*, Long Beach Art Museum, Long Beach, California. (catalogue)
1973   *Newport Harbor Art Museum, Newport Beach, California.
1975   *Abstraction: Alive and Well*, State University College, Potsdam, New York.
1976   *Women's Interart Center, New York.
1977   *The Proscenium: The Staged Words of Ida Applebroog, Manny Farber and Patricia Patterson*, P.S. 1, Long Island City, New York.
1978   *Whitney Museum of American Art, New York.
1979   *Williams College Museum of Art, Williamstown, Massachusetts.
        *Franklin Furnace, New York. (manuscript)
1980   *Rotterdam Arts Foundation, Rotterdam.
1981   *Ronald Feldman Fine Arts, New York.
        *Gallerie il Diagramma, Milan.
        *Galleria del Cavallino, Venice, Italy. (catalogue)
1982   *Nigel Greenwood Gallery, London.
        Current Events, Ronald Feldman Fine Arts, New York.
1983   *Spectacolor Board*, Times Square, New York.
        Common Causes, Koplin Gallery, Los Angeles.
        Directions 83, Hirshhorn Museum and Sculpture Garden, Smithsonian Institution, Washington, D.C. (catalogue)

1984   *Carl Solway Gallery, Cincinnati.
        *Anderson Gallery, Virginia Commonwealth University, Richmond.
        *Castillo Gallery, New York.
        *Chrysler Museum, Norfolk, Virginia.
        Inmates and Others, Ronald Feldman Fine Arts, New York.
        Artist's Call Against U.S. Intervention in Central America, P.S. 1, Long Island City, New York.
1985   *Galleria del Cavallino, Venice, Italy.
        *Dart Gallery, Chicago.
1986   *Cul de Sacs*, Ronald Feldman Fine Arts, New York.
        Investigations, ICA, University of Pennsylvania, Philadelphia.
1987   *Wadsworth Atheneum, Matrix Gallery, Hartford, Connecticut
        *Ronald Feldman Fine Arts, New York.
1988   *Reed College, Portland, Oregon.
1989   *Art at the Edge: Ida Applebroog*, High Museum of Art, Atlanta. Traveled to Carnegie Mellon Art Gallery, Pittsburgh. (catalogue)
        Nostrums, Ronald Feldman Fine Arts, New York. (catalogue)
1990   *Happy Families*, Contemporary Arts Museum, Houston. Traveled to the Power Plant, Toronto. (catalogue)
        *Seed Hall, Seibu, Tokyo. (catalogue)
1991   *Galerie Langer Fain, Paris.
        *Avtozavodskaya, Moscow. (catalogue)
        *Barbara Gross Galerie, Munich.
        *Ulmer Museum, Ulm, Germany. Traveled to Bonner Kunstverein, Bonn and NGBK Berlin. (catalogue)
        Safety Zone, Ronald Feldman Gallery, New York.
1992   *Stichting de Appel, Amsterdam.
1993   *Weatherspoon Art Gallery, University of North Carolina, Greensboro. (catalogue)
        *Gallery Paule Anglim, San Francisco.
        *Orchard Gallery, Derry, Ireland. Traveled to Irish Museum of Modern Art, Dublin. (catalogue)
        Whitney Biennial, Whitney Museum of American Art, New York. (catalogue)
        43rd Biennial Exhibition of Contemporary American Painting, Corcoran Gallery of Art, Washington, D.C. (catalogue)

Bibliography

Ashbery, John. "Biennials Blooming in the Spring." *Newsweek:* April 18, 1983. 93–94.
Atkins, Robert. "Scene and Heard." *Village Voice:* April 30, 1991. 45–46.
Brach, Paul. "Ida Applebroog at Ronald Feldman." *Art in America:* February 1983. 139–140.
Brenson, Michael. "Art People: Sculpture 'Speaks Out' at Downtown Landmark." *New York Times:* November 12, 1982. C25.
_____. "The Social Club." *New York Times:* January 22, 1988. C24.
Cameron, Dan. "Against Collaboration." *Arts:* March 1984.
_____. "Illustration is Back in the Picture." *ARTnews:* November 1985. 114–120.
_____. "Report from the Front." *Arts:* Summer 1986. 86.
Gambrell, Jamey. "Ida Applebroog at Feldman." *Art in America:* January 1985. 141–142.
Gill, Susan. *ARTnews:* April 1986. 154–155.
Gimelson, Deborah. "The Show the Art World Loves to Hate." *Mirabella:* March 1993. 82–85.
Glueck, Grace. "A New Showcase for Art by Women." *New York Times:* April 1, 1988.
_____. *New York Times:* October 26, 1984.
Heartney, Eleanor. "Ida Applebroog." *ARTnews:* January 1988. 151–152.
Hess, Elizabeth. "Art of the State." *Village Voice:* February 16, 1988. 39–41.
_____. "Art + Politics = Biennial—Up Against the Wall." *Village Voice:* March 16, 1993.
Linker, Kate. "Ida Applebroog." *Artforum:* January 1988. 109–110.
Princenthal, Nancy. "Ida Applebroog at Ronald Feldman." *Art in America:* February 1988.
Raven, Arlene. "Not a Pretty Picture." *Village Voice:* June 17, 1986. 98.
Schjeldahl, Peter. "Art + Politics = Biennial—Missing: The Pleasure Principle." *Village Voice:* March 16, 1993.
Schor, Mira. "Medusa Redux, Ida Applebroog and the Spaces of Post-Modernity." *Artforum:* March 1990. 116–122.
Smith, Roberta. "Americana with Benign and Sinister Side by Side." *New York Times:* November 1, 1991.
Wallach, Amei. "Art With an Attitude." *New York Newsday:* March 5, 1993. 52–53.

KEN APTEKAR

Born 1950, Detroit, Michigan
Lives New York City

Education

1973   University of Michigan, Ann Arbor, (BFA)
1975   Pratt Institute, Brooklyn, New York (MFA)

Fellowships and Awards

1980   Artists Space Grant-in-Aid
1987   National Endowment for the Arts
1989   Pollock-Krasner Foundation
1991   Djerassi Foundation Residency
1992   Ucross Foundation Residency
        Rockefeller Foundation Residency,
        Bellagio, Italy

Selected Exhibitions

1977   *2nd International Festival of Avant-Garde
        Cinema*, Caracas, Venezuela.
1978   Franklin Furnace, New York.
1979   Art Latitude Gallery, New York.
1980   Art Galaxy, New York.
1981   *Five Photographers*, Midtown Y Gallery,
        New York.
1982   *What I Do For Art*, Just Above
        Midtown/Downtown, New York.
1983   *On View*, New Museum of Contemporary
        Art, New York.
1984   *Sid Deutsch Gallery, New York.
1986   Art In General, New York.
1987   *The Other Man*, New Museum, New
        York. (catalogue)
1989   *Bess Cutler Gallery, New York.
        Gender Fictions, SUNY-Binghamton Art
        Museum, Binghamton, New York.
        Serious Fun, Truthful Lies, Randolph
        Street Gallery, Chicago.
1990   *Margulies-Taplin Gallery, North Miami.
        Post-Boys and Girls: Nine Painters,
        Artists Space, New York.
        Critical Revisions, Bess Cutler Gallery,
        New York.
        June 4, 1989, China, P.S. 1, Long Island
        City, New York.
        In Bloom, organized by the Museum of
        Modern Art for Pfizer, Inc., New York.
1991   *New Generation: New York*, Carnegie
        Mellon University Art Museum,
        Pittsburgh. (catalogue)
        Drawing Time, Newhouse Center For
        Contemporary Art, Snug Harbor, Staten
        Island.
1992   *Decoding Gender*, P.S. 33, Baltimore.
1993   *43rd Biennial Exhibition of Contemporary
        American Painting*, Corcoran Gallery of
        Art, Washington, D.C. (catalogue)

82

Bibliography

Atkins, Robert. "New This Week: Ken Aptekar."
Seven Days: December 5, 1989.
Glueck, Grace. "Critics' Choices," *New York
Times:* June 20, 1982.
Henry, Gerrit. "Ken Aptekar at Bess Cutler." *Art in
America:* June 1990.
Hess, Elizabeth. "Yesterday's Children." *Village
Voice:* December 4, 1990.
McCracken, David. "Exhibit Has Its Fun and Its
Serious Sides." *Chicago Tribune:* March 10, 1989.
Raynor, Vivien. "'Bedrooms' and Drawings." *New
York Times:* February 17, 1991.
Saslow, James. "Rethinking Masculinity: Ken
Aptekar." *The Advocate:* May 22, 1990.
Shortal, Helen. "Bodily Fluids: School 33
Deconstructs the Birds and the Bees." *City Paper:*
March 6, 1992.
Zimmer, William. "Ken Aptekar." *SoHo Weekly
News:* November 22, 1979.
_____. "Kenneth Aptekar at Sid
Deutsch." *Arts:* May 1984.

DOTTY ATTIE

Born 1938, Pennsauken, New Jersey
Lives New York City

Education

1959   College of Art, Philadelphia (BFA)
1960   Brooklyn Museum, Beckman Fellowship

Fellowships and Awards

1973   Creative Artists Public Service Grant
1975   National Endowment for the Arts
1976   Creative Artists Public Service Grant
1981   Childe Hassam Purchase Grant
1982   Hassam/Speicher Purchase Grant
1983   National Endowment for the Arts
1985   Creative Artist Fellowship for Japan
1987   Mid-Atlantic States Residency

Selected Exhibitions

1972   *A.I.R. Gallery, New York.
1973   *Artists Books*, Moore College of Art,
        Philadelphia.
1974   *Stockton State College, Pomona, New
        Jersey.
        *A.I.R. Gallery, New York.
1975   *Five Americans*, Galerie Gerald Piltzer,
        Paris.
1976   *A.I.R. Gallery, New York.
1977   *O.K. Harris Gallery, New York.
1978   *A.I.R. Gallery, New York.
        Narration, Institute of Contemporary Art,
        Boston. (catalogue)
1979   *Dotty Attie; Drawing 1975/79*,
        Contemporary Arts Museum, Houston.
        (catalogue)
        Directions I, Hirshhorn Museum and
        Sculpture Garden, Smithsonian
        Institution, Washington, D.C. (catalogue)
1980   *Wadsworth Atheneum, Hartford,
        Connecticut.
        *Portland Center for Visual Artists,
        Portland, Oregon.
        *A.I.R. Gallery, New York.
1981   *Pennsylvania Academy of Fine Arts,
        Philadelphia.
        New Dimensions In Drawing, Aldrich
        Museum, Ridgefield, Connecticut.
        (catalogue)
1982   *Norton Gallery and School of Art, Palm
        Beach, Florida.
        *A.I.R. Gallery, New York.
1983   *Ackland Art Museum, Chapel Hill, North
        Carolina.
        *New Museum of Contemporary Art,
        New York.
        *A.I.R. Gallery, New York.
1984   *Bowdoin College Museum of Art,
        Brunswick, Maine.
        *Dotty Attie: Masters of Contemporary
        Drawing*, Virginia Commonwealth
        University, Richmond. (catalogue)

1985   *Sanat Gallery, Istanbul, Turkey.
        Dotty Attie/The Mechanical Peep Show,
        Valencia Community College, Orlando,
        Florida. (catalogue)
1986   *On Gallery, Osaka, Japan.
        *A.I.R. Gallery, New York.
1987   *Works From the Collection*, National
        Museum of Women in the Arts,
        Washington, D.C. (catalogue)
        Ten Major Women Artists, Rockland
        Center For the Arts, Washington, D.C.
1988   *P.P.O.W., New York.
1989   *Pittsburgh Center for the Arts,
        Pittsburgh. (catalogue)
        Five Tales, University of Missouri, St.
        Louis.
1990   *Greenville County Museum of Art,
        Greenville, South Carolina.
        *P.P.O.W., New York.
        *Tyler School of Art, Temple University,
        Philadelphia.
        Referees, North Carolina Museum of Art,
        Raleigh. (catalogue)
1991   *In the Atelier*, P.P.O.W., New York.
        *Galerie Rizzo and Hubbard, Paris.
1992   *The Frame: Multiplied and Extended*,
        Security Pacific Gallery, Costa Mesa,
        California.
1993   *43rd Biennial Exhibition of Contemporary
        American Painting*, Corcoran Gallery of
        Art, Washington, D.C. (catalogue)

Bibliography

Alloway, Lawrence. *The Nation:* May 14, 1974.
Ashbery, John. *New York:* July 2, 1979.
Berger, Maurice. "The Empty Frame." *Arts:*
September 1981.
Bourdon, David. *Art in America:* March/April 1977.
Cotter, Holland. *Art in America:* December
1988. 149.
Kozloff, Max. "The Discreet Voyeur." *Art in
America:* July 1991. 100–106, 137.
Kuspit, Donald. *Art in America:* February 1984.
_____. *Artforum:* December 1988. 117.
Larson, Kay. *New York:* November 24, 1980.
Levin, Kim. *Village Voice:* April 3, 1985.
Perreault, John. *Village Voice:* December 28, 1972.
Raynor, Vivien. *New York Times:* November 1980.
_____. *New York Times:* November 1984.
Robins, Corrine. "Changing Stories." *Arts:*
November 1988. 80–85.
_____. "Dotty Attie: Narrative as
Ordered Nightmare." *Arts:* November 1976.
Russell, John. *New York Times:* June 11, 1976.
Smith, Roberta. *Arts:* January 1973.

LUIS CRUZ AZACETA

Born 1942, Havana, Cuba
Lives New Orleans

Education

1969   School of Visual Arts, New York

Fellowships and Awards

1972   Cintas Foundation, New York
1975   Cintas Foundation, New York
1980   National Endowment for the Arts
1981   Creative Artists Public Service Grant
1984   Canadian Club Hispanic Award
1985   National Endowment For the Arts
        Guggenheim Foundation Grant
        New York Foundation for the Arts
1989   Mid-Atlantic States Fellowship
1991   National Endowment for the Arts
        Penny McCall Foundation Award

Selected Exhibitions

1975   *New Talent*, Allan Frumkin Gallery.
1978   *Allan Frumkin Gallery, Chicago.
        *Cayman Gallery, New York.
1979   *Allan Frumkin Gallery, New York.
1981   *Richard L. Nelson Gallery, University of
        California, Davis.
        *Candy Store, Folsom, California.
        Crimes of Compassion, Chrysler Museum,
        Norfolk, Virginia.
        Emerging Artists, Alternative Museum,
        New York. (catalogue)
1982   *Allan Frumkin Gallery, New York.
1983   *Apocalypse and Utopia*, Moravian
        College, Bethlehem, Pennsylvania.
        (catalogue)
        Inside Self Someone Else, Dayton Art
        Institute, Dayton, Ohio. (catalogue)
1984   *Allan Frumkin Gallery, New York.
        (catalogue)
        *Candy Store, Folsom, California.
1985   *Allan Frumkin Gallery, New York.
        American Artists of Cuban Origins,
        Miami-Dade Community College, South
        Campus, Florida. (catalogue)
1986   *Allan Frumkin Gallery, New York.
        *Candy Store, Folsom, California.
        *Anderson Gallery, Virginia
        Commonwealth University, Richmond.
        *Museum of Contemporary Hispanic Art,
        New York. (catalogue)
1987   *Gallery Paule Anglim, San Francisco.
        Tough Ride Around the City, Fondo del
        Sol Visual Arts Center, Washington, D.C.
        (catalogue)
        *Contemporary Hispanic Art in the United
        States*. Traveling exhibition organized by
        the Corcoran Gallery of Art, Washington,
        D.C. (catalogue)

1988   *Frumkin/Adams Gallery, New York.
        *Kunst Station, Cologne, West Germany.
        (catalogue)
        Committed to Print, Museum of Modern
        Art, New York. (catalogue)
1989   *Frumkin/Adams Gallery, New York.
        (catalogue)
        *Opus Art studios, Inc., Coral Gables,
        Florida. (catalogue)
1990   *Frumkin/Adams Gallery, New York.
        (catalogue)
        * *The AIDS Epidemic Series*. Traveling ex-
        hibition organized by the Queens
        Museum, New York. (catalogue)
        *VII Bienal Iberoamericana de Arte—
        Caracteres de Identidad en Pueblos
        IberoAmericanos*, Museo de Arte
        Moderno, Mexico. (catalogue)
        The Decade Show, New Museum of
        Contemporary Art; Museum of
        Contemporary Hispanic Art; and the
        Studio Museum, New York. (catalogue)
1991   *Frumkin/Adams Gallery, New York.
        * *Obras Selectas: Trayectoria*, Galeria
        Botello, Hato Rey, Puerto Rico.
        (catalogue)
        15 Artistas Cubanos, Galeria Ninart,
        Mexico City. (catalogue)
1992   *Frumkin/Adams Gallery, New York.
        *Picturing the World Turned Upside Down:
        Paintings by Luis Cruz Azaceta*, Galeria
        Ramis Barquet, Monterrey, Mexico.
        (catalogue)
        *Selections From the 'AIDS Epidemic'
        Series*, Rhode Island School of Design,
        Providence, Rhode Island.
1993   * *Identity and Chaos*, Daniel Saxon
        Gallery, Los Angeles.
        *43rd Biennial Exhibition of Contemporary
        American Painting*, Corcoran Gallery of
        Art, Washington, D.C. (catalogue)

Bibliography

Baker, Kenneth. "Luis Cruz Azaceta." *San Francisco Chronicle:* March 27, 1987.
Glueck, Grace. "Of Beasts and Humans: Some Contemporary Views." *New York Times:* November 14, 1982.
_____. *New York Times:* January 27, 1984.
Hagen, Charles. "All That Jazz." *ARTnews:* February 1990. 112–117.
Kessler, Pamela. "Crocodiles on the Subway." *Washington Post:* April 24, 1987.
McGreevy, Linda. "Painting His Heart Out: The Work of Luis Cruz Azaceta." *Arts:* Summer 1985.
Raynor, Vivien. "Art: Resurgence in El Barrio." *New York Times:* April 28, 1978.
_____. "Art Divided Exhibition Presents Old As New." *New York Times:* January 4, 1985.
Richard, Paul. "In a Cuba State of Mind; Tri-Venue Show Reflects Yearnings of a Lost Homeland." *Washington Post:* May 26, 1991.
Smith, Roberta. "Art: 67 Years of Works by Latin Americans." *New York Times:* November 13, 1987.
Zimmer, William. "A Latin American 'Salad Bowl' at the Jersey City Museum." *New York Times:* May 18, 1986.

DONALD BAECHLER

Born 1956, Hartford, Connecticut
Lives New York City

Education

1977   College of Art, Maryland Institute,
        Baltimore
1978   Cooper Union, New York
1979   Staatliche Hochschule fur bildende
        Kunste, Frankfurt

Selected Exhibitions

1975   Wadsworth Atheneum, Hartford,
        Connecticut.
1977   *Maryland Institute, Baltimore.
1978   *Arts Tower, Baltimore.
1979   *Galerie Patio, Frankfurt/M, Germany.
        *P.S. 33, Baltimore.
1980   *Artists Space, New York.
1981   *Numerosette-Galleria N'apoletana delle
        Arti, Naples, Italy.
1982   *Hallwalls, Buffalo, New York.
        The Human Figure, Contemporary Arts
        Center, New Orleans. (catalogue)
1983   *Tony Shafrazi, New York. (catalogue)
1984   *Neue Bilder, Ascan Crone, Hamburg.
        *Tony Shafrazi, New York.
        Works on Paper, Galerie Peter Pakesch,
        Vienna.
        Behind Faces and Figures, Philadelphia
        College of Art.
1985   *Pat Hearn Gallery, New York.
        *Hamburger Gemälde, Ascan Crone,
        Hamburg. (catalogue)
1986   *Akira Ikeda, Nagoya, Japan. (catalogue)
        *Larry Gagosian, Los Angeles.
        *Malningar, Teckningar, Grafik, Anders
        Tornberg, Lund, Sweden.
1987   *Tony Shafrazi, New York.
        Terrae Motus, Grand Palais, Paris.
        XIX Bienal de São Paolo. (catalogue)
1988   *Donald Baechler Paintings and
        Drawings: 1982–1987, Illinois State
        University, Normal. Traveled to Virginia
        Commonwealth University, Richmond,
        Virginia. (catalogue)
        *Anders Tornberg, Lund, Sweden.
1989   *Paul Kasmin, New York.
        *Tony Shafrazi, New York.
        *Recent Etchings, Baron/Boisante
        Editions, New York.
        *Flowers and Trees, Lars Bohman,
        Stockholm.
        *E+O Friedrich, Bern.
        Et Museum for Moderne Kunst i Malmö
        Kunsthallen Brandts Klaederfabrik,
        Malmö, Sweden.
        Whitney Biennial, Whitney Museum of
        American Art, New York. (catalogue)

1990   *Gian Enzo Sperone, Rome.
        *New Prints 1990, AC&T Corp., Tokyo.
        (catalogue)
        *Works on Paper, Paul Kasmin, New
        York.
        *New Prints, Baron/Boisante Editions,
        New York.
        *Greenberg Gallery, St. Louis, Missouri.
        *Paintings, Bronzes and Works on Paper,
        Tony Shafrazi, New York.
        About Round/Round About, Anders
        Tornberg, Lund, Sweden.
        The Last Decade: American Artists of the
        '80's, Tony Shafrazi, New York.
        (catalogue)
1991   *Luhring Augustine Hetzler, Santa
        Monica, California.
        *James Corcoran Gallery, Santa Monica,
        California.
        *Max Hetzler, Cologne.
        *Collagen, Gisela Capitain, Cologne.
        *Anders Tornberg, Lund, Sweden.
        *Paintings of 1981 + 1982,
        Baron/Boisante, New York.
        *E+O Friedrich, Bern.
        *Kunst-Station, Cologne.
1992   *Pedro Oliveira, Porto, Portugal.
        *Gian Enzo Sperone, Rome.
        Regard Multiple, Centre Pompidou, Paris.
        Drawings, Stuart Regen, Los Angeles.
1993   Floor Show Sculptures and Objects,
        Anders Tornberg Gallery, Lund Sweden.
        Tutte le strade portano a Roma? Achille
        Bonito Oliva and Comune di Roma, Rome.
        43rd Biennial Exhibition of Contemporary
        American Painting, Corcoran Gallery of
        Art, Washington, D.C. (catalogue)

Bibliography

Adams, Brooks. Art in America: September 1985.
141.
Cotter, Holland. "New York: Donald Baechler at
Tony Shafrazi." Art in America: April 1986. 187.
Ellis, Stephen. "Donald Baechler at Paul Kasmin
and Tony Shafrazi." Art in America: June 1989.
170–171.
Kuspit, Donald. Artforum: June 1983. 80.
Levin, Kim. "Drawing." Village Voice: February 10,
1982.
Mahoney, Robert. Arts: February 1986.
Morgan, Stuart. Artscribe: December
1985/January 1986. 60–61.
Ratcliff, Carter. "Notes on Line." Art in America:
June 1990. 152–157.
Russell, John. "The Secret Life of Art is Lead in
Drawings." New York Times: Sunday, June 28,
1992.
Saunders, Wade. "Making Art Making Artists."
Art in America: January 1993. 80–81.
Smith, Roberta. New York Times: Friday, April 10,
1987.
_____. New York Times: Friday, March
25, 1988.
_____. "More Women and Unknowns in
the Whitney Biennial." New York Times: Friday,
April 28, 1989.
Steenhuis, Paul. "Donald Baechler 'Mondrian met
een pik.'" Mitropolis M #6: Jan/Feb 1984. 47–49.

MICHAEL BYRON

Born 1954, Providence, Rhode Island
Lives Amsterdam, The Netherlands

Education

1976   Kansas City Art Institute (BFA)
1981   Nova Scotia College of Art and Design,
        Halifax (MFA)

Fellowships and Awards

1989   National Endowment for the Arts

Selected Exhibitions

1982   *For the Nun*, Artists Space, New York.
        The Crucifix Show, Barbara Gladstone
        Gallery, New York.
        The Beast, P.S. 1 Museum, Long Island
        City, New York.
1983   *White Columns, New York.
        Travels Afoot, Gallery Nature Morte,
        New York.
        *Lawrence Oliver Gallery, Philadelphia.
        Hundreds of Drawings, Artists Space,
        New York.
1984   *Willard Gallery, New York.
        Dramatic Dimensions, Hallwalls, Buffalo.
        *New Work: Inside New York/Outside
        New York*, New Museum of
        Contemporary Art, New York. (catalogue)
        *An International Survey of Recent
        Painting and Sculpture*, Museum of
        Modern Art, New York. (catalogue)
        A Few Fears, Tyler School of Art, Temple
        University, Philadelphia.
1985   *Working Drawings and One Candle*,
        Nova Scotia College of Art and Design,
        Halifax, Nova Scotia.
        Spanish Titles, Lawrence Oliver Gallery,
        Philadelphia.
        Actual Size, Larry Gagosian Gallery,
        Los Angeles.
1986   *Luhring, Augustine and Hodes Gallery,
        New York.
        Byron-Kessler, Galerie Barbara Farber,
        Amsterdam.
1987   *Mario Diacono, Boston.
        *Galerie Barbara Farber, Amsterdam.
        *Aldrich Museum of Contemporary Art,
        Ridgefield, Connecticut.
1988   *Luhring, Augustine and Hodges Gallery,
        New York.
        Social Spaces, Artists Space, New York.
        (catalogue)
1989   *Phyllis Kind Gallery, Chicago.
        *Galerie Barbara Farber, Amsterdam.
        Whitney Biennial, Whitney Museum of
        American Art, New York. (catalogue)

1990   *Baron/Boisante Gallery, New York.
        *Galerie Gisela Capitain, Cologne.
        (catalogue)
        *Luhring Augustine Hetzler, Santa
        Monica, California.
        Against the Grain, Whitney Museum of
        American Art, Stamford, Connecticut.
        (catalogue)
1991   *Anders Tornberg, Lund, Sweden.
        *Baron/Boisante Gallery, New York.
        *Witte de With, Rotterdam. (catalogue)
        *Boymans-van Beuningen Museum,
        Rotterdam. (catalogue)
        Elga Wimmer, New York. (catalogue)
1992   *Galerie Barbara Farber, Amsterdam.
        *Anders Tornberg Gallery, Lund, Sweden.
        Recent Acquisitions and Donations,
        Whitney Museum of Art, New York.
        Phoenix Art Museum, Phoenix.
1993   *Elga Wimmer, New York. (catalogue)
        *Baron/Boisante, New York.
        *Philippe Gravier, Paris. (catalogue)
        *43rd Biennial Exhibition of Contemporary
        American Painting*, Corcoran Gallery of
        Art, Washington, D.C. (catalogue)

Bibliography

Cotter, Holland. "Michael Byron at Luhring,
Augustine & Hodes Gallery." *Art in America*:
December 1986.
Knight, Christopher. "Byron: Disguise, Desire and
Deception." *Los Angeles Times*: September 14,
1990.
Leigh, Christian. "Michael Byron." *Artforum*: May
1988.
Levin, Kim. "Michael Byron." *Village Voice*: June
3, 1986.
_____. "The Permanent Point of View."
Village Voice: May 22, 1984.
O'Brien, Glenn. "Beat." *Interview*: April 1986.
Smith, Roberta. "Social Spaces." *New York
Times*: Friday, February 12, 1988.
Van Beek, Willem. "Michael Byron, John
Kessler." *Kunstbeeld*: March 1986.
Welling, Wouter. "Het Poetische Theater van
Michael Byron." *Kunstbeeld*: 1991.
Wingen, Ed. "Het Theater van Michael Byron."
Kunstbeeld: February 1987.

DREW BEATTIE & DANIEL DAVIDSON

DREW BEATTIE

Born 1952, Atlanta
Lives Berkeley, California

Education

1974   University of North Carolina, Chapel Hill
        (BFA)
1978   School of the Museum of Fine Arts,
        Boston (MFA)

DANIEL DAVIDSON

Born 1965, San Francisco
Lives San Francisco

Education

1990   San Francisco Art Institute (BFA)

Selected Exhibitions

1990   *Stephen Wirtz Gallery, San Francisco.
1992   *Gallery Paule Anglim, San Francisco.
        One By Two, Artists in Collaboration,
        Sonoma State University, Rohnert Park,
        California.
1993   *Gallery Paule Anglim, San Francisco
        *Germans Van Eck, New York.
        Selections/Spring '93, The Drawing
        Center, New York.
        *43rd Biennial Exhibition of Contemporary
        American Painting*, Corcoran Gallery of
        Art, Washington, D.C. (catalogue)

Bibliography

Baker, Kenneth. "Shows Illustrate the 'Why' and 'How' of Painting." *San Francisco Chronicle:* March 14, 1992.
_____. "Painters Team Up on Playful Canvases." *San Francisco Chronicle:* June 16, 1990.
Cebulski, Frank. "Drew Beattie and Daniel Davidson." *Artweek:* July 19, 1990.

PHYLLIS BRAMSON

Born 1941, Madison, Wisconsin
Lives Chicago

Education

1962   Yale University, Art Scholarship
1963   University of Illinois (BFA)
1964   University of Wisconsin (MA)
1974   School of the Art Institute of Chicago
        (MFA)

Fellowships and Awards

1976   National Endowment for the Arts
1980   Louis Comfort Tiffany Foundation
1981   Illinois Arts Council
1983   National Endowment for the Arts
1988   Fulbright Fellowship
        Illinois Arts Council Fellowship
1993   Guggenheim Fellowship
        Marie Walsh Sharpe New York City
        Studio Grant

Selected Exhibitions

1976   *Artemisia Gallery, Chicago.
        Object as Poet, Renwick Gallery,
        Smithsonian Institution, Washington,
        D.C.
1977   *Monique Knowlton Gallery, Chicago.
1978   *Marianne Deson Gallery, Chicago.
        Mayor Daley's Tomb, NAME Gallery,
        Chicago.
1979   *Monique Knowlton Gallery, New York.
        Installation Drawings, New Museum of
        Contemporary Art, New York. (catalogue)
1980   *Dart Gallery, Chicago.
        Chicago/Chicago, Contemporary Art
        Center, Cincinnati. (catalogue)
1981   *Monique Knowlton Gallery, New York.
        (catalogue)
        Prints and Multiples, Art Institute of
        Chicago. Traveled to National Academy
        of Design, New York; Illinois State
        Museum, Springfield; National Museum
        of American Art, Washington, D.C.
1982   *Monique Knowlton Gallery, New York.
1983   *Marilyn Butler Gallery, Scottsdale,
        Arizona.
        *Dart Gallery, Chicago.
1984   *Seigfried Gallery, Athens, Ohio.
        *Monique Knowlton Gallery, New York.
1985   *Dart Gallery, Chicago.
        *Joseph Gross Gallery, University of
        Arizona, Tucson.
        *Hewlett Gallery, Carnegie-Mellon
        University, Pittsburgh.

1986   *Renaissance Society at the University of
        Chicago (catalogue)
1987   *College of DuPage, Glen Ellyn, Illinois.
        *Brody's Gallery, Washington, D.C.
        Paintings and Drawings 1973–1986,
        Illinois Wesleyan University,
        Bloomington.
        Phyllis Bramson: Imagist, Parkland
        College, Champaign, Illinois.
1988   *Dart Gallery, Chicago.
        *Victorian College of the Arts,
        Melbourne, Australia.
        *Lake View Museum of Art and Sciences,
        Peoria, Illinois.
        *Southern Illinois University at
        Carbondale.
        *The Developing Images: Continuity and
        Change in a Chicago Artistic Tradition*,
        Jonson Gallery, University of New
        Mexico, Albuquerque.
1990   *Locations of Desire*, Illinois State
        Museum, Springfield. (catalogue)
1991   *Judith Racht Gallery, Harbert, Michigan.
        *Douglass College/Rutgers University,
        New Brunswick, New Jersey.
1992   *Dart Gallery, Chicago.
1993   *Brody's Gallery, Washington, D.C.
        *43rd Biennial Exhibition of Contemporary
        American Painting*, Corcoran Gallery of
        Art, Washington, D.C. (catalogue)

Bibliography

Butera, Virginia F. "Phyllis Bramson." *Arts:* May
1982.
Condon, Elizabeth. "Phyllis Bramson at Dart
Gallery." *New Art Examiner:* May 1992.
Frueh, Joanna. "Phyllis Bramson at the
Renaissance Society." *Art in America:* September
1986.
_____. "Phyllis Bramson at Monique
Knowlton." *Art in America:* January 1980.
Larson, Kay. "Imperialism with a Grain of Salt."
Village Voice: September 17, 1979.
_____. "Primal Dreams." *New York:*
March 26, 1984.
McCracken, David. "3 Artists Cast a Critical View
at Exhibition." *Chicago Tribune:* February 12, 1988.
Morrison, C.L. "Phyllis Bramson at Marianne
Deson Gallery." *Artforum:* April 1978. 72–73.
Raynor, Vivien. "Phyllis Bramson." *New York
Times:* May 23, 1986.
Rickey, Carrie. "Chicago." *Art in America:*
July/August 1978.
_____. "Put the Blame on Boys, Mame."
Village Voice: November 2, 1982.
Russell, John. "Phyllis Bramson at Monique
Knowlton." *New York Times:* March 12, 1982.
Westerbeck, Cody. "Phyllis Bramson." *Artforum:*
Summer 1986.
Yood, James. "Phyllis Bramson at Dart Gallery."
Artforum: May 1992.

CAROLE CAROOMPAS

Born 1946, Oregon City, Oregon
Lives Los Angeles

Education

1968   California State University (BA)
1971   University of Southern California (MFA)

Fellowships and Awards

1987   National Endowment for the Arts
1989   New School of Social Research,
        New York

Selected Exhibitions

1972   *Southern California Attitudes*, Pasadena
        Museum of Art, Pasadena, California.
        (catalogue)
        The Last Plastics Show, Cal Arts,
        Valencia, California. (catalogue)
        Survivors 72, Henry Gallery, University of
        Washington, Seattle.
1974   *Women Artists*, Cal State University,
        Fresno, California. (catalogue)
        24 from LA, Municipal Art Gallery,
        Los Angeles. (catalogue)
1976   *Los Angeles—New Work*, Museum of
        Modern Art, New York.
        Autobiographical Fantasies, Los Angeles
        Institute of Contemporary Art, Los
        Angeles. (catalogue)
1977   *Ellie Blankfort Gallery, Los Angeles.
        Maps, Museum of Modern Art,
        New York.
        Surrogate and Self, Holly Solomon
        Gallery, New York. (catalogue)
1978   *Jan Baum Gallery, Los Angeles,
        California.
        Art About Art, Whitney Museum of
        American Art, New York. (catalogue)
        From Self-Portrait to Autobiography,
        Neuberger Museum, Purchase, New
        York. (catalogue)
1979   *Carole Caroompas and Nancy Truax*,
        Wordworks, San Jose, California.
1980   **The Songs She Sang to Herself*, LAICA,
        Los Angeles.
        *Jan Baum Gallery, Los Angeles,
        California.
1981   *Mapped Art: Charts, Routes and Regions*,
        University of Colorado, Boulder.
        (catalogue)
        *Decade: Los Angeles Painting in the
        Seventies*, Art Center College of Design,
        Pasadena, California. (catalogue)
        Words as Images, Renaissance Society at
        the University of Chicago. (catalogue)

1982   *Jan Baum Gallery, Los Angeles.
        *The Michael and Dorothy Blankfort
        Collection*, Los Angeles County Museum
        of Art (catalogue)
1983   **Carole Caroompas—A Survey
        1972–1983*, California State University,
        Northridge (catalogue)
        *Jan Baum Gallery, Los Angeles.
1984   *California Bookworks: The Last Five
        years*, Otis Art Institute of Parsons School
        of Design, Los Angeles. (catalogue)
        Olympiad: Summer '84, Koplin Gallery,
        Los Angeles.
1985   *Karl Bornstein Gallery, Los Angeles.
1986   *A Southern Californian Collection*, Cirrus
        Gallery, Los Angeles. (catalogue)
        Hollywood Inside and Out, Municipal Art
        Gallery, Los Angeles.
1987   *Passages: A Survey of California Women
        Artists 1945–Present*, Fresno Art
        Museum, Fresno, California.
1988   *Book Exhibition*, LACE, Los Angeles.
        20 Artists/Los Angeles, City Gallery of
        Contemporary Art, Raleigh, North
        Carolina. (catalogue)
1989   *Los Angeles Contemporary Exhibitions,
        Los Angeles. (catalogue)
        Pasadena Armory Show, The Armory,
        Pasadena, California. (catalogue)
1990   *Fine Arts Gallery, University of
        California, Irvine. (catalogue)
        Faces, Marc Richards Gallery,
        Los Angeles.
1991   *Go Figure: New Painting of the Human
        Image*, College Art Gallery, Pasadena,
        California. (catalogue)
        Addictions, Contemporary Arts Forum,
        Santa Barbara, California. (catalogue)
1992   *Sue Spaid Fine Art, Los Angeles.
        (catalogue)
        LA-Exhibitions, Municipal Art Gallery, Los
        Angeles. (catalogue)
1993   P.P.O.W., New York.
        *43rd Biennial Exhibition of Contemporary
        American Painting*, Corcoran Gallery of
        Art, Washington, D.C. (catalogue)

Bibliography

Anderson, Michael. *Art in America:* April 1990.
Clothier, Peter. *Art in America:* Summer 1980.
Gabrielson, Walter. "Pasadena Pluralism." *Art in
America:* May 1981.
Gardner, Colin. *Los Angeles Times:* August 11,
1986.
Marmer, Nancy. *Artforum:* April 1976.
Pagel, David. "Southern Attitudes." *Los Angeles
Times:* June 19, 1992.
Plagens, Peter. "Southern Cal. Attitudes."
Artforum: February 1973.
Tager, Alisa. "The Girls Issue." *Tema Celeste:*
September 1992.
Weissman, Benjamin. *Artforum:* March 1990.

ROBERT COLESCOTT

Born 1925, Oakland, California
Lives Tucson, Arizona

Education

1949 University of California, Berkeley (BA)
1952 University of California, Berkeley (MA)

Fellowships and Awards

1964 American Research Center, Egypt
1976 National Endowment for the Arts
1980 National Endowment for the Arts
1983 National Endowment for the Arts
1985 Guggenheim Foundation
1987 Residency, Roswell, New Mexico
1989 Residency, Tamarind Institute

Selected Exhibitions

1950 Salon de Mai, Paris.
1958 *Portland Art Museum, Portland, Oregon.
1960 *Portland Art Museum, Portland, Oregon.
1961 *Reed College, Portland, Oregon.
1968 *21 Peintres Americains*, Musée D'Angouleme, France.
1969 *Trois Americains*, Centre Culturel Americain, Paris.
1972 *Friedlander Gallery, Seattle.
1974 *Third World Exhibit*, San Francisco Museum of Modern Art.
1975 *Razor Gallery, New York.
1977 *Razor Gallery, New York.
Painting and Sculpture in California, San Francisco Museum of Modern Art. Traveled to National Collection of Fine Arts, Washington, D.C.
1978 *John Berggruen Gallery, San Francisco.
Art About Art, Whitney Museum of American Art, New York. (catalogue)
1979 *Hamilton Gallery, New York.
1980 *The Bay Area—Colescott, Brown, and DeForest*, Fountain Gallery, Portland, Oregon.
1982 *Semaphore Gallery, New York.
1983 *Freedman Gallery, Albright College, Reading, Pennsylvania.
Second Western States Exhibition; 38th Corcoran Biennial Exhibition of American Painting. Traveling exhibition organized by the Corcoran Gallery of Art, Washington, D.C. (catalogue)
1984 *Content: A Contemporary Focus 1974–1984*, Hirshhorn Museum and Sculpture Garden, Smithsonian Institution, Washington, D.C. (catalogue)
Confrontations, Henry Art Gallery, University of Washington, Seattle.
The Human Condition, San Francisco Museum of Modern Art.

1985 *At The Bathers' Pool*, Semaphore Gallery, New York.
Another Judgement, Knight Gallery, Charlotte, North Carolina.
*Semaphore Gallery, New York.
Here and Now, Greenville County Museum of Art, Greenville, South Carolina.
The Artist and The Model, ICA, University of Pennsylvania, Philadelphia.
1986 *Les Demoiselles D'Alabama*, Semaphore Gallery, New York.
*Koplin Gallery, Los Angeles.
1987 *Phyllis Kind Gallery, Chicago.
*Semaphore Gallery, New York.
*Rena Bransten Gallery, San Francisco.
Robert Colescott: A Retrospective, 1975–1986. Traveling exhibition organized by the San Jose Museum of Art, San Jose, California. (catalogue)
1988 *Koplin Gallery, Los Angeles.
1989 *Robert Colescott, A Retrospective*, Seattle Art Museum. (catalogue)
*Phyllis Kind Gallery, New York.
The Blues Aesthetic: Black Culture and Modernism, Washington Project for the Arts, Washington, D.C. (catalogue)
1990 *Howard Yezerski Gallery, Boston.
*Linda Cathcart Gallery, Los Angeles.
*Phyllis Kind Gallery, Chicago.
*Arthur Roger Gallery, New Orleans.
1991 *Phyllis Kind Gallery, New York.
*University of Colorado, Boulder.
The Decade Show, New Museum of Contemporary Art; Museum of Hispanic Art; and the Studio Museum Harlem, New York. (catalogue)
1992 *Phyllis Kind Gallery, New York and Chicago.
1993 *Phyllis Kind Gallery, New York.
*Linda Cathcart Gallery, Santa Monica, California.
I Am the Enunciator, Thread Waxing Space, New York. (catalogue)
43rd Biennial Exhibition of Contemporary American Painting, Corcoran Gallery of Art, Washington, D.C. (catalogue)

Bibliography

Adams, Brooks. "Robert Colescott at Phyllis Kind." *Art in America:* July 1991.
Atkins, Robert. "Satirical Sass." *Elle:* March 1989.
Baker, Kenneth. "Bay Area Alums on L.A. Scene." *San Francisco Chronicle:* May 8, 1986.
Becker, Robert. "Art: Satiric Mastery—Robert Colescott." *Interview:* December 1983. 141–143.
Brenson, Michael. "Black Artists: A Place in the Sun." *New York Times:* Sunday, March 12, 1989.
Douglas, Robert L. "Robert Colescott's Searing Stereotypes." *New Art Examiner:* June 1989. 34–37.
Ferguson, Bruce W. "Reading Rights and Writing Wrongs." *Artforum:* May 1993.
Glueck, Grace. "Two Biennials: One Looking East and the Other West." *New York Times:* March 27, 1983.
Hirsh, Faye. "L'ecole de Paris is Burning: Robert Colescott's Ironic Variations." *Arts:* September 1991. 52–57.
Johnson, Ken. "Colescott on Black and White." *Art in America:* June 1989. 148–153.
Larson, Kay. *New York:* March 13, 1989.
Levin, Kim. "Art Pick." *Village Voice:* May 1, 1984.
Plagens, Peter. "The Academy of the Bad." *Art in America:* November 1981.
Ratcliff, Carter. "The Distractions of Theme." *Art in America:* November 1981.
Raynor, Vivien. *New York Times:* April 6, 1984.
Richard, Paul. "Robert Colescott's Perspectives on Black and White." *Washington Post:* January 20, 1988.
Russell, John. "Robert Colescott at Semaphore Gallery." *New York Times:* April 6, 1984.
Schjeldahl, Peter. "But Seriously Folks..." *Village Voice:* December 9, 1981.
Sims, Lowrey S. "Bob Colescott Ain't Misbehavin'" *Artforum:* March 1984. 56–59.
—————. "The Mirror The Other: The Politics of Esthetics." *Artforum:* March 1990.
Smith, Roberta. "The Whitney Biennial—Taking Consensus," *Village Voice:* April 26, 1983.
Zimmer, William. "Political Messages." *New York Times:* October 1985.

KIM DINGLE

Born 1951, Pomona, California
Lives Los Angeles

Education

1988   California State University, Los Angeles
       (BFA)
1990   Claremont Graduate School, Claremont,
       California (MFA)

Selected Exhibitions

1990   *Con-Text*, Richard/Bennett Gallery,
       Los Angeles.
1991   **Dingle Library Presents Paintings of the
       West with Horse Drawings by Teenage
       Girls*, Richard/Bennett Gallery,
       Los Angeles.
       **Portraits from the Dingle Library*,
       Richard/Bennett Gallery, Los Angeles.
       **The Romance and Drama of the Rubber
       Industry*, Closet of Modern Art, California
       State University, Los Angeles.
       Synthetic Histories, Parker/Zanic Gallery,
       Los Angeles.
       Over the Couch, Boritzer/Gray Gallery,
       Santa Monica, California.
       Les Fleurs, Parker/Zanic Gallery, Los
       Angeles.
       The Store Show, Richard/Bennett Gallery,
       Los Angeles.
1992   *Kim Light Gallery, Los Angeles.
       *I Thought California Would be Different:
       New Work in the Permanent Collection*,
       Laguna Art Museum, Laguna Beach,
       California.
1993   *43rd Biennial Exhibition of Contemporary
       American Painting*, Corcoran Gallery of
       Art, Washington, D.C. (catalogue)

Bibliography

Curtis, Cathy. "Hers is Unfinished Business." *Los
Angeles Times:* September 23, 1992.
Crocket, Toby. *Art in America:* July 1992.
Kandel, Susan. "Skewed Portraits." *Los Angeles
Times:* September 12, 1991.
Pagel, David. "Kim Dingle." *Arts:* December 1991.
Frank, Peter. "Pick of the Week." *L.A. Weekly:*
November 12, 1990.

INGA FRICK

Born 1951, Los Angeles
Lives Washington, D.C.

Education

1976   Cabrillo College, Aptos, California (AS)
1978–   University of California at Santa Cruz
1981   (BA, BFA)
1985   University of Pennsylvania (MFA)

Fellowships and Awards

1981   Chancellor's Award, UC Santa Cruz
1982   Scholarship Award, University of
        Pennsylvania
1988   Maryland State Arts Council
1989   Fairfax County Council of the Arts
        Prince George's County Arts Council
        Maryland Arts Place
1990   Prince George's County Arts Council
1991   Prince George's County Arts Council

Selected Exhibitions

1978   *Oakes College Gallery, Santa Cruz,
        California.
1980   Stevenson College Gallery, Santa Cruz,
        California.
1982   *Santa Cruz Art Center, Santa Cruz,
        California.
1985   *Alumni Show*, Sesnon Gallery,
        Santa Cruz, California.
        Alternative Solutions, Zenith Gallery,
        Washington, D.C.
        MFA Show, ICA, University of
        Pennsylvania, Philadelphia.
1987   *BACA Downtown, Brooklyn, New York.
        Art Where It Lives, Creative Metalworks,
        Washington, D.C.
1989   *Rosenberg Gallery, Goucher College,
        Towson, Maryland.
        Open Exhibition 1989, Fairfax County
        Judicial Center, Fairfax, Virginia.
        Arlington Art Center, Arlington, Virginia.
1990   *Middendorf Gallery, Washington, D.C.
        Art Against Aids, Washington, D.C.
        City Visions, Harbor Place and the
        Gallery, Baltimore, Maryland.
1991   Middendorf Gallery, Washington, D.C.
1992   *Cardinal Gallery, Annapolis, Maryland.
        Willow Street Gallery, Washington, D.C.
        *Montpelier Cultural Arts Center, Laurel,
        Maryland.
1993   *Jones Troyer Fitzpatrick Gallery,
        Washington, D.C.
        *Lingua Pittura: Painting's Evolving
        Agendas*, McLean Project for the Arts,
        Arlington, Virginia. (brochure)
        *43rd Biennial Exhibition of Contemporary
        American Painting*, Corcoran Gallery of
        Art, Washington, D.C. (catalogue)

Bibliography

Avasthi, Surabhi. "Ardor in the Court."
McLean/Great Falls Connection: March 30, 1989.
Corcoran, Leila. "Regional Art Exhibit Reflects
Styles." *McLean Providence Journal:* March 16,
1989.
Gauss, Robert. *Santa Cruz Sentinel:* February 7,
1982.
Hsuan, A.B. "BACA Shows the State of the Art in
Williamsburg." *The Brooklyn Phoenix:* July 30,
1987.
Jackson, Jonathan D. "Do Read Between the
Lines." *Quindecim:* September 15, 1989.
Lance, Amy. *Eyewash:* October 1992.
Lyon, Ellen. "Frick Exhibit Opens at Montpelier."
Prince Georges Sentinel: October 15, 1992.
Mahoney, James. *Art in America:* May 1993. 128.
Miller, Eric. "Paintings by Inga Frick and John R.
Viles." *The Alternative:* September 1989.
Segnan, Pat. *Eyewash:* June 1990.

CHARLES GARABEDIAN

Born 1923 Detroit, Michigan
Lives Santa Monica, California

Education

1961   University of California at Los Angeles
        (MA)

Fellowships and Awards

1977   National Endowment for the Arts
1980   Guggenheim Fellowship

Selected Exhibitions

1962   *Four Painters*, Cejee Gallery, Los Angeles.
1965   *Cejee Gallery, Los Angeles.
1966   *La Jolla Museum of Art, La Jolla,
        California.
        *Cejee Gallery, Los Angeles.
1967   *Cejee Gallery, Los Angeles.
1974   *California State University at
        Northridge. (catalogue)
1975   *University of California, Santa Barbara
        Whitney Biennial, Whitney Museum of
        American Art, New York. (catalogue)
1976   *Whitney Museum of American Art, New
        York. (catalogue)
        XXXVII Venice Biennale, American
        Pavilion, Venice, Italy.
        *Painting and Sculpture in California,
        Modern Art*, San Francisco Museum of
        Modern Art. Traveled to National
        Collection of Fine Arts, Smithsonian
        Institute, Washington, D.C. (catalogue)
1977   *American River College, Sacramento,
        California.
1978   *Bad Painting*, New Museum of
        Contemporary Art, New York. (catalogue)
1979   *L.A. Louver Gallery, Venice, California.
1980   *Collage and Ceramic Works: 1978–80*,
        L.A. Louver, Venice, California.
1981   *Just a Great Thing to Do: Selected
        Works by Charles Garabedian*, La Jolla
        Museum of Contemporary Art, La Jolla,
        California.
1983   *Painting 1978–1982*, L.A. Louver Gallery,
        Venice, California. (catalogue)
        Twenty Years of Work, Rose Art
        Museum, Waltham, Massachusetts.
        (catalogue)
        The First Show, Museum of Contemporary
        Art, Los Angeles. (catalogue)

1984   *Hirschl & Adler Modern, New York.
        (catalogue)
        *Content: A Contemporary Focus,
        1974–1984*, Hirshhorn Museum and
        Sculpture Garden, Smithsonian
        Institution, Washington, D.C. (catalogue)
        First Newport Biennial, Newport Harbor
        Art Museum, Newport Beach, California.
        (catalogue)
        *Paradise Lost/Paradise Regained,
        American Visions of the New Decade*,
        41st Venice Biennale, U.S. Pavilion.
        Traveling exhibition organized by the
        New Museum of Contemporary Art,
        New York. (catalogue)
1985   *Gallery Paule Anglim, San Francisco.
        *Arts Club of Chicago. (catalogue)
        The Figure in 20th-Century American Art.
        Traveling exhibition organized by the
        Metropolitan Museum of Art, New York.
        Whitney Biennial, Whitney Museum of
        American Art, New York. (catalogue)
1986   *Tunneling Backwards*, L.A. Louver,
        Venice, California.
        *Individuals: A Selected History of
        Contemporary Art, 1945–1986*, Museum
        of Contemporary Art, Los Angeles.
        (catalogue)
1987   *Hirschl & Adler Modern, New York.
        Ten at the Rose, Rose Art Museum,
        Brandeis University, Waltham,
        Massachusetts. (catalogue)
1988   *New York Work: 1984–1987*, L.A.
        Louver, Venice, California.
1989   *Projects and Portfolios: Twenty-Fifth
        Annual Print Exhibition*, Brooklyn
        Museum of Art, New York.
1990   *...loyal Athenians flock down to the
        seashore with cooking-pots in which they
        stew different kinds of beans...*
        L.A. Louver, Venice, California.
1991   *L.A. When it Began*, James Corcoran
        Gallery, Los Angeles.
1992   *Studies for the Iliad*, L.A. Louver, Venice,
        California, and Louver Gallery, New York.
1993   *Studies for the Iliad*, Gallery Paule
        Anglim, San Francisco.
        *43rd Biennial Exhibition of Contemporary
        American Painting*, Corcoran Gallery of
        Art, Washington, D.C. (catalogue)

Bibliography

Armstrong, Richard. *Artforum:* March 1983.
French, Christopher. "An Austere Passion."
Artweek: October 26, 1985.
Henry, G. *Art in America:* January 1993.
Hoffman, Fred. *Art in America:* 1980.
Kessler, C. "Newspace." *Art in America:* May 1975.
_____. "Fragile Sledgehammer of
Garabedian: Whitney Museum of American Art."
Arts: February 1976.
Larsen, Susan. "First Newport Biennial."
ARTnews: February 1985.
Picot, Pierre. "The Search for Understanding."
Artweek: March 4, 1989.
Schipper, M. *ARTnews:* April 1986.
Weissman, B. *Artforum:* April 1990.
Yau, John. *Art in America:* October 1983.

93

LEON GOLUB

Born 1922, Chicago
Lives New York City

Education

1949   School of the Art Institute of Chicago
        (BFA)

Fellowships and Awards

1954   Art Institute of Chicago
1960   Ford Foundation
1962   Art Institute of Chicago, Purchase Prize
1967   Cassandra Foundation
1968   Guggenheim Foundation
1986   Art Institute of Chicago

Selected Exhibitions

1947   *First Veterans Annual*, School of the Art
        Institute of Chicago.
1950   *Contemporary Gallery, Chicago.
1954   *Artists Gallery, New York.
        Carnegie International, Pittsburgh.
1955   *Allan Frumkin Gallery, Chicago.
1956   *Pasadena Museum of Art, Pasadena,
        Califronia.
        Annual Exhibition, Whitney Museum of
        American Art, New York.
1962   *Corcoran Annual*, Corcoran Gallery of Art,
        Washington, D.C.
1964   Documenta III, Kassel, West Germany.
1966   *University of Chicago.
1967   *Le Monde en Question*, Musée d'Art
        Moderne, Paris.
1968   *The Obsessive Image, 1960–68*, Institute
        of Contemporary Art, London.
1969   *El Bienial International del Deporte en las
        Bellas Artes*, Madrid.
1970   *National Gallery of Victoria, Melbourne.
1972   *Political Prisoners*, Berkeley, California.
1974   *Museum of Contemporary Art, Chicago.
1975   *New York Cultural Center.
1976   *San Francisco Art Institute.
1977   *Memorial to Orlando Letelier*, Cayman
        Gallery, New York.
1978   *Colgate University, Colgate, New York.
1979   *School of Visual Arts, New York.
1980   *American Figurative Painting 1950–1980*,
        Chrysler Museum, Norfolk, Virginia.
1981   *The Figure in American Art*, Museum of
        Southwest Texas, Corpus Christi.
1982   *Susan Caldwell, Inc., New York.

1983   *Honolulu Academy of Arts, Honolulu,
        Hawaii.
        **Matrix/Berkeley 58*, Art Museum,
        University of California at Berkeley.
        *Leon Golub: *Mercenaries, Interrogations
        and Other Works*. Traveling exhibition or-
        ganized by the University of Houston,
        Texas.
        Whitney Biennial, Whitney Museum of
        American Art, New York. (catalogue)
1984   *Galerie Darthea Speyer, Paris.
        **Golub*. Traveling exhibition organized by
        the New Museum of Contemporary Art,
        New York. (catalogue)
1985   **Currents*, Institute of Contemporary Art,
        Boston.
1986   *Barbara Gladstone Gallery, New York.
        **Leon Golub/Nancy Spero*, Greenville
        County Museum of Art, Greenville, South
        Carolina.
1987   *Kunstmuseum, Lucerne, Switzerland.
        (catalogue)
        Documenta 8, Kassel, West Germany.
1988   *Barbara Gladstone Gallery, New York.
        *Saatchi Collection, London.
        *Galerie Neuendorf, Frankfurt.
        Committed to Print, Museum of Modern
        Art, New York. (catalogue)
1989   *Eli Broad Family Foundation,
        Los Angeles.
        *Rhona Hoffman Gallery, Chicago.
        *Burnett Miller Gallery, Los Angeles.
        *Cranbrook Academy of Art, Bloomfield
        Hills, Michigan.
1990   *Josh Baer Gallery, New York.
        The Decade Show, New Museum of
        Contemporary Art; Museum of
        Contemporary Hispanic Art; and the
        Studio Museum of Harlem, New York.
1991   **WorldWide*, Brooklyn Museum,
        Brooklyn, New York.
1992   *Patriots, Josh Baer Gallery, New York.
        *Musée D'Art Contemporaine de
        Montreal, Quebec.
        **Paintings 1987–92*, ICA, University of
        Pennsylvania, Philadelphia. (catalogue)
        *Parallel Visions: Modern Artists and
        Outsider Art*, Los Angeles County
        Museum of Art. (catalogue)
1993   **Leon Golub/Nancy Spero*, Josh Baer
        Gallery, New York.
        *Malmö, Sweden. (catalogue)
        *43rd Biennial Exhibition of Contemporary
        American Painting*, Corcoran Gallery of
        Art, Washington, D.C. (catalogue)

Bibliography

Adrian, Dennis. "Leon Golub Returns Home in All His Crushing Power." *Chicago Daily News:* September 8, 1974.

Alloway, Lawrence. "Leon Golub: Art & Politics." *Artforum:* October 1974. 66–71.

_____. "Art," *The Nation:* February 19, 1977.

Avgikos, Jan. "'Patriots' at Josh Baer Gallery." *Artforum:* April 1992.

Baigell, Matthew. "The Mercenaries: An Interview with Leon Golub." *Arts:* May 1981. 167–169.

Brenson, Michael. "Art: From Leon Golub, Political Thugs Gallery." *New York Times:* February 10, 1984.

Brooks, Rosetta. "Undercover Agent." *Artforum:* January 1990. 114–121.

Dreiss, Joseph. "Leon Golub's Gigantomachies: Permagon Revisited." *Arts:* May 1981.

French, Christopher. "The Voice of Outrage," *Artweek:* March 19, 1983. 1.

Hess, Elizabeth. "The Killing Fields." *Village Voice:* December 13, 1988.

Hughes, Robert. "The Human Clay in Extremis." *Time:* December 31, 1984.

Kuspit, Donald. "Golub's Assassins: An Anatomy of Violence." *Art in America:* May/June 1975.

Levin, Kim. "Power to the Painter." *Village Voice:* February 28, 1984.

Lippard, Lucy. "Making Manifest." *Village Voice:* January 27, 1982.

Marzorati, Gerald. "A Painter of Darkness: Leon Golub and Our Times": *Viking Penguin, Inc.*, New York, 1990.

Ratcliff, Carter. "Theater of Power." *Art in America:* January 1984. 74–82.

Rosenberg, Harold. "Aesthetics of Mutilation." *New Yorker:* May 12, 1975.

Storr, Robert. "Riddled Sphinxes." *Art in America:* March 1989. 126–131.

Wei, Lily. "On Nationality: 13 Artists." *Art in America:* September 1991.

CATHERINE HOWE

Born 1959, Williamsville, New York
Lives New York City

Education

1982   State University of New York at Buffalo
        (BFA)
1984   State University of New York at Buffalo
        (MFA)

Selected Exhibitions

1984   *Nine Painters,* Hallwalls, Buffalo.
1985   Hallwalls, Buffalo.
1987   White Columns, New York.
1988   *Contention,* New Langton Arts,
        San Francisco.
        *Romantic Distance (or absence makes
        the heart grow fonder),* Jeffrey Neale
        Gallery, New York.
        The Wayward Muse, Albright-Knox
        Gallery, Buffalo.
1989   *Invitational Exhibition,* Albright-Knox Art
        Gallery, Buffalo, New York. (catalogue)
        Topical Rain Forest, Red Square,
        New York.
1990   **Special Projects,* P.S. 1, Long Island City,
        New York.
        Conflict of Image, Soho Center,
        New York.
        Althea Viafora Gallery, New York.
1991   *Stephanie Theodore Gallery, New York.
        House of Value, 252 Lafayette Street,
        New York.
        Preview '91, Stephanie Theodore Gallery.
1992   *Stephanie Theodore Gallery, New York.
        Boy Meets Girl, Horodner Romley Gallery,
        New York.
        10 Steps, Muranushi Lederman Gallery,
        New York.
        The Anti-Masculine, Kim Light Gallery,
        Los Angeles.
1993   *Johan Jonker Gallery, Amsterdam.
        (catalogue)
        *Elizabeth Koury Gallery, New York.
        All Too Human, Stiebel Modern,
        New York.
        The Irony and the Ecstacy, Salama-Caro
        Gallery, London. (catalogue)
        Image/Abstraction, Amy Lipton Gallery,
        New York.
        *43rd Biennial Exhibition of Contemporary
        American Painting,* Corcoran Gallery of
        Art, Washington, D.C. (catalogue)

Bibliography

Mahoney, Robert. *Arts:* May 1991.
Smith, Roberta. "The New Appropriationists."
New York Times: August 16, 1992.
_____. "New Galleries in Soho..." *New
York Times:* November 15, 1991.
Zinsser, John. "Losses in Translation." *Arts:*
October 1990.

DAVID HUMPHREY

Born 1955, Pittsburgh
Lives New York City

Education

1977   Maryland Institute College of Art,
        Baltimore (BA)
1980   New York University, New York (MA)

Fellowships and Awards

1980   Creative Artists Public Service Grant
1985   New York Council for the Arts
1987   National Endowment for the Arts

Selected Exhibitions

1979   *Washington Square Gallery, New York.
1980   State University of New York at
        Purchase.
1981   *Thirty New York Painters*, Hobart College,
        Geneva, New York.
1982   *New Talent*, Alpha Gallery, Boston.
        Summer Show, David McKee Gallery,
        New York.
1983   *Pittsburgh Plan For Art, Pittsburgh.
1984   *David McKee Gallery, New York.
        *Intermedia: Between Painting and
        Sculpture*, Aldrich Museum of Contem-
        porary Art, Ridgefield, Connecticut.
        A Refocus on Landscape, P.S. 33,
        Baltimore.
1985   *David McKee Gallery, New York.
        Artists in Two Mediums, Bennington
        College Art Gallery, Bennington, Vermont.
        Art in the Anchorage, Creative Time,
        Brooklyn, New York.
1986   *American Art Today: The Figure in the
        Landscape,* Florida International
        University, Miami.
        *Public and Private: American Prints
        Today*, Brooklyn Museum, Brooklyn, New
        York. (catalogue)
        The Potent Image, Morris Museum of Art,
        Morristown, New Jersey.
        (catalogue)
1987   *Rena Bransten Gallery, San Francisco.
        *Drawings from the 80's—Chatsworth
        Collection*, Carnegie Mellon University,
        Pittsburgh.
1988   *David McKee Gallery, New York.
        (catalogue)
        *Alpha Gallery, Boston.
        Fresh from New York, Artspace,
        Auckland, New Zealand. (catalogue)
1989   *Krygier/Landau Contemporary Art, Santa
        Monica, California.

1990   *Krygier/Landau Contemporary Art, Santa
        Monica, California.
        *David McKee Gallery, New York.
        The Unique Print: 70's into the 90's,
        Museum of Fine Arts, Boston.
        (catalogue)
1991   *Bergstrom-Mahler Museum, Neenah,
        Wisconsin. (catalogue)
        *Rena Bransten Gallery, San Francisco.
        *McKee Gallery, New York.
        Landscape as Stage, Locks Gallery,
        Philadelphia. (catalogue)
1992   *Dysfunction in the Family Album*, Diane
        Brown Gallery, New York.
        (Drawing) Pictures, P.S. 1, Long Island
        City, New York.
        Hair, John Michael Kohler Arts Center,
        Sheboygan, Wisconsin.
1993   *Appraising the Preternatural*, Patricia
        Shea Gallery, Santa Monica, California.
        Pittsburgh Collects, Carnegie Institute,
        Pittsburgh.
        Psychological Impact, Northampton
        Community College, Bethlehem,
        Pennsylvania.
        *43rd Biennial Exhibition of Contemporary
        American Painting*, Corcoran Gallery of
        Art, Washington, D.C. (catalogue)

Bibliography

Baker, Kenneth. "David Humphrey." *Art in
America:* January 1985.
_____. "David Humphrey: Walk on the
Weird Side." *San Francisco Chronicle:* February 9,
1991.
Cohn, Ronnie. "David Humphrey." *ARTnews:*
December 1984.
Cyphers, Peggy. *Arts:* September 1991.
Levin, Kim. "David Humphrey-Centerfold." *Village
Voice:* October 22, 1985.
Cotter, Holland. "David Humphrey." *Flash Art:*
December 1985.
_____. "David Humphrey." *Art in
America:* September 1988.
Gardner, Colin. "Galleries." *Los Angeles Times:*
May 2, 1986.
Hagen, Charles. "Dysfunction in the Family
Album." *New York Times:* January 31, 1992.
Homes, A.M. "Dysfunction in the Family Album."
Artforum: May 1992.
Regan, Kate. "David Humphrey." *ARTnews:*
Summer 1987.
Welsman, Benjamin. "David Humphrey-Patricia
Shea Gallery." *Artforum:* November 1992.
Yau, John. "David Humphrey." *Artforum:* May
1988.

HUNG LIU

Born 1948, Changchun, China
Lives Oakland, California

Education

1975   Beijing Teachers College (BFA)
1981   Central Academy of Fine Art, Beijing
        (MFA)
1986   University of California, San Diego (MFA)

Fellowships and Awards

1985   Research Grant, University of California,
        San Diego
1986   Graduate Student Research Grant,
        University of California, San Diego
1988   Capp Street Project
1989   National Endowment for the Arts
1991   Public Art Commission, Moscone
        Convention Center, San Francisco
        National Endowment for the Arts
1993   Fleishhacher Foundation

Selected Exhibitions

1978   *Portraiture Exhibition*, Winter Palace
        Gallery, Beijing.
1981   *The Music of the Great Earth*, perma-
        nent mural, Central Academy of Fine Arts,
        Beijing.
1985   *Grotto Variations*, Sheppard Fine Arts
        Gallery, University of Nevada, Reno.
1986   *Up and Tao*, permanent mural,
        University of California, San Diego.
1987   *Once there were Ten Suns...*, D-Art
        Visual Art Center, South Dallas Cultural
        Center, Dallas.
        Combinations, Bath House Cultural
        Center, Dallas.
        UTA Faculty: New Work, University of
        Texas at Arlington.
1988   *Figures*, Brazos Gallery, Richard College,
        Dallas.
        Reading Room, Capp Street Project at
        the Community Room of Chinese for
        Affirmative Action, Chinatown,
        San Francisco.
        Resident Alien, Capp Street Project, San
        Francisco.
        Where is Mao?, Southwestern College
        Art Gallery, Chula Vista, California.
1989   *Where is Mao?*, version II, Brown-
        Lupton Gallery, Texas Christian
        University, Fort Worth, Texas.
        Trauma, Sushi Gallery, San Diego,
        California.
        Chinese Pieta, The Woman's Building,
        Los Angeles.
        Goddess of Love and Liberty, Nathan
        Contemporary Gallery, New York.

1990   *Trauma, 1989*, Diverse-Works, Houston.
        Contemporary Art by Women of Color,
        Hemisfair Plaza, San Antonio, Texas.
        *Precarious Links: Emily Jennings, Hung
        Liu, Celia Munoz*, San Antonio Museum
        of Art, San Antonio, Texas. Traveled to
        Lawndale Art and Performance Center,
        Houston.
        *Narrative Constructs—Contemporary
        Trends by Women Artists of Color*,
        Women and Their Work Gallery,
        Austin, Texas.
        Official Language, Walter McBean
        Gallery, San Francisco Art Institute.
1991   *Rena Bransten Gallery*, San Francisco.
        Mito y Magia En America: Los Ochenta,
        Museum of Contemporary Art,
        Monterrey, Mexico.
        Counter Colon-ialismo, Centro Cultural de
        la Raza, San Diego, California.
        Selected Bay Area Drawings, Drawing
        Center, New York. Traveled to Pro Arts,
        Oakland, California.
        Viewpoints: Eight Installations, Richmond
        Art Center, Richmond, California.
        Disparate: Seven Workers, Upaya
        Gallery, San Francisco.
1992   *Bernice Steinbaum Gallery, New York.
        Decoding Gender, P.S. 33, Baltimore.
        Why Painting-Part 1, Susan Cummins
        Gallery, Mill Valley, California.
1993   *Backtalk*, Santa Barbara Contemporary
        Arts Forum, Santa Barbara, California.
        (catalogue)
        Eureka Award Winners, San Jose
        Museum of Art, San Jose, California.
        *43rd Biennial Exhibition of Contemporary
        American Painting*, Corcoran Gallery of
        Art, Washington, D.C. (catalogue)

Bibliography

Baker, Kenneth. "A Proper Women's Show at
Transamerica." *San Francisco Chronicle:* May 11,
1991.
Bonetti, David. "Shades of Misogyny, Facism."
San Francisco Examiner: November 22, 1991.
Ennis, Michael. "The Ties that Bind." *Texas
Monthly:* September 1990.
Goddard, Dan R. "SAMA Exhibit Studies Cultural
Ties." *Express-News: San Antonio*, July 15, 1990.
Kutner, Janet. "A New Spark For the City's
Modern Art." *Dallas Morning News:* May 20, 1990.
Lippard, Lucy R. "Mixed Blessings." *Pantheon
Books: New York*, October 1990.
Nyo, Paula Tin. "No Pencils." *Artweek:* April 25,
1991.
Oleson, J.R. "Feminism Colors New Collection."
Austin-American Statesman: September 22, 1990.
Pellecchia, Michael. "Texas Exodus." *Dallas
Observer:* July 19, 1990.
Rapko, John. "Modes of Seeing." *Artweek:*
November 8, 1990.
Roche, Harry. "Global Disconnection." *Artweek:*
November 8, 1990.
Smith, Irvin. "Disparate: Seven Workers."
Artweek: April 25, 1991.
Thomas, Sherry Lee. "A World of Difference."
Artweek: May 9, 1991.
Tyson, Janet. "This 'Vessel' Carries the Goods."
Fort Worth Star-Telegram: June 29, 1990.
Watten, Barrett. "The Powers of Imbalance."
Artweek: November 28, 1991.
Weser, Marcia Goren. "Trio's Exhibit Shows Ties
That Bind Women." *San Antonio Light:* July 7,
1990.
Zinsser, John. "Hung Liu at Nahan
Contemporary." *Art in America:* June 1990.

JIM LUTES

Born 1955, Fort Lewis, Washington
Lives Chicago

Education

1978   Washington State University (BA)
1982   School of the Art Institute of Chicago
       (MFA)

Fellowships and Awards

1974   Pischel Award
1976   Balliet Scholarship, Washington State
       University
1981   Anna Louise Rauymond Traveling
       Fellowship
1985   Illinois Arts Council Grant
1987   SECCA Awards in the Visual Arts 7

Selected Exhibitions

1977   *Pedestrian Art, Pullman, Washington.
1978   Off the Wall, Gallery II, Pullman,
       Washington.
1983   Emerging, Renaissance Society at the
       University of Chicago.
       Jim Lutes/Jin Soo Kim, Randolph Street
       Gallery, Chicago.
1984   Chicago 1984: Artists to Watch, Dart
       Gallery, Chicago.
       Chicago and Vicinity, Art Institute of
       Chicago.
       39th Corcoran Biennial of Contemporary
       American Painting, Corcoran Gallery of
       Art, Washington, D.C. (catalogue)
1985   Viewpoints: Doug Argue/Jim Lutes,
       Walker Art Center, Minneapolis.
       (catalogue)
1986   *Dart Gallery, Chicago.
       Recent Art From Chicago, Artists Space,
       New York. (catalogue)
1987   *Dart Gallery, Chicago.
       Whitney Biennial, Whitney Museum of
       American Art, New York. (catalogue)
       Surfaces: Two Decades of Painting in
       Chicago, Terra Museum of American Art,
       Chicago.
1988   *Dart Gallery, Chicago.
       SECCA Awards in the Visual Arts 7.
       Traveling exhibition organized by the
       Southeastern Center for Contemporary
       Arts, Winston-Salem, North Carolina.
       Art and Democracy, Group Material, DIA
       Foundation, New York.

1989   *Michael Kohn Gallery, Los Angeles.
       *Forms of Contemporary Illinois, Illinois
       State Museum, Springfield and State of
       Illinois Gallery, Chicago.
       Chicago Artists in the European Tradition,
       Museum of Contemporary Art, Chicago.
       Encore—Celebrating Fifty Years,
       Contemporary Arts Center, Cincinnati.
1990   *Temple Gallery, Tyler School of Art,
       Philadelphia.
       *University of Missouri, St. Louis.
       Ponton, Temse, Belgium.
1991   *Dart Gallery, Chicago.
       *LedisFlam Gallery, New York.
       Spirited Visions, State of Illinois Art
       Gallery, Chicago. (catalogue)
1992   *Dart Gallery, Chicago.
       *Susan Bitter-Larkin Gallery, New York.
       Documenta IX, Kassel, Germany.
       (catalogue)
       Why Paint?, Renaissance Society at the
       University of Chicago. (catalogue)
       Face to Face; Self-Portraits by Chicago
       Artists, Cultural Center, Chicago.
1993   43rd Biennial Exhibition of Contemporary
       American Painting, Corcoran Gallery of
       Art, Washington, D.C. (catalogue)

Bibliography

Adrian, Dennis. "Two Decades of Painting in
Chicago." New Art Examiner: December 1987.
Artner, Alan G. "Is Painting Dead?" Chicago
Tribune: April 1992. 16–17.
Bonesteel, Michael. "Report from the Midwest:
39th Corcoran Biennial: The Death Knell of
Regionalism?" Art in America: October 1985.
31–37.
Bulka, Michael. New Art Examiner: March 1991.
Curtis, Cathy. "Jim Lutes." Los Angeles Times:
August 4, 1989.
Hixson, Kathryn. Arts: April 1991, 107–108.
_____. "Jim Lutes." Arts: December 1988.
Indiana, Gary. "Another Review of the Whitney."
Village Voice: April 28, 1987.
McCormick, Carlo. "Jim Lutes: Fat Chances."
Artforum: December 1988.
Neff, Eileen. "Jim Lutes: Temple Gallery."
Artforum: December 1990.
Pagel, David. "Art Pick of the Week—Jim Lutes."
Los Angeles Times: August 18, 1989.
Richard, Paul. "Funny, Figurative and Fierce."
Washington Post: February 1985.
Riddle, Mason. "Doug Argue/Jim Lutes." New
Art Examiner: April 1986.
Taylor, Sue. "Jim Lutes." Art in America: April
1990.

KERRY JAMES MARSHALL

Born 1955, Birmingham, Alabama
Lives Chicago

Education

1977   Los Angeles City College
1978   Otis Art Institute, Los Angeles (BFA)

Fellowships and Awards

1985   Studio Museum at Harlem, New York.
1990   Art Matters Inc.
1991   National Endowment for the Arts

Selected Exhibitions

1984   *Pepperdine University Art Gallery,
        Malibu, California.
        James Turcotte Gallery, Los Angeles.
        Faculty Exhibition, Los Angeles
        Southwest College Art Gallery, Los
        Angeles.
        Olympiad, Summer '84, Koplin Gallery,
        Los Angeles.
        The Finals in Painting and Sculpture, Jan
        Baum Gallery, Los Angeles.
        Environs 3, Loyola Law School Gallery,
        Los Angeles.
        Artist's Call, Thinking Eye Gallery, Los
        Angeles.
        Seventeen Self-Portraits by L.A. Artists,
        Occidental College, Los Angeles.
1985   *Koplin Gallery, Los Angeles.
        Fusion '85, Jewish Federation Council,
        Los Angeles.
        Purchase Show, Santa Monica Artbank,
        Santa Monica, California.
        The Spiritual Eye, Loyola Law School
        Gallery, Los Angeles.
        The Floor Show, LACE, Los Angeles.
        *Fifth Annual Afro-American Artists
        Exhibition*, Atlanta Life Insurance Co.,
        Atlanta.
1986   *Home for the Holidays*, Koplin Gallery,
        Los Angeles.
        Two Person Group Show, Studio Museum
        at Harlem, New York.
        Only Los Angeles, Municipal Art Gallery,
        Los Angeles.
1991   *Koplin Gallery, Santa Monica,
        California.
        Drawings, Koplin Gallery, Santa Monica.
1992   *Social Figuration*, San Diego State
        University, San Diego, California.
        Black & White, Art Alliance Gallery,
        Riverside, California.
        God's Violent World: Artists Respond,
        Elmhurst College, Elmhurst, Illinois.
        *Dreams & Demons: Modern Mythic
        Visions*, Evanston Art Center, Evanston,
        Illinois.
1993   *Koplin Gallery, Santa Monica,
        California.
        *Jack Shainman Gallery, New York.
        *43rd Biennial Exhibition of Contemporary
        American Painting*, Corcoran Gallery of
        Art, Washington, D.C. (catalogue)

Bibliography

Kennedy, Shawn. "For Fledgling Artists, A Place
to Grow." *New York Times:* June 18, 1986.
McKenna, Kristine. "Mixed Media Hommage to
Black Martyr." *Los Angeles Times:* March 15, 1991.
Pincus, Robert. *Los Angeles Times:* October 14,
1983.
Smith, Roberta. "Kerry James Marshall at Jack
Shainman Gallery," *New York Times:* February 12,
1993.
Yau, John. "Kerry James Marshall at Jack
Shainman Gallery," *Artforum:* May 1993.

MELISSA MILLER

Born 1951, Houston, Texas
Lives Austin, Texas

Education

1969– University of Texas, Austin
1971

1971 Museum of Fine Arts School, Houston
1974 Yale Summer School of Music and Art
1974 University of New Mexico (BFA)

Fellowships and Awards

1974 Yale Summer School of Music and Art
1979 National Endowment for the Arts
1982 National Endowment for the Arts
      Ann Giles Kimbrough Fund, Dallas
      Museum of Art
1985 National Endowment for the Arts
1987 Texas Art Award

Selected Exhibitions

1973 A.S.A. Gallery, University of New Mexico,
      Albuquerque.
1974 Southwest Fine Arts Biennial, Museum of
      New Mexico, Santa Fe.
1977 *Women and Their Work*, Laguna Gloria
      Museum, Austin, Texas.
1978 *Young Artists Series*, Amarillo Art
      Center, Amarillo, Texas. (catalogue)
1979 *Vital Signs*, Aperture Gallery, Austin,
      Texas.
1980 *Texas Only*, Laguna Gloria Art Museum,
      Austin, Texas.
      New Orleans Triennial, New Orleans
      Museum of Art. (catalogue)
1981 *Projects Gallery, Art Museum of South
      Texas, Corpus Christi.
      *Perspectives Gallery, Contemporary Arts
      Museum, Houston. (catalogue)
1983 *Texas Gallery, Houston.
      Texas Images and Visions, Archer M.
      Huntington Gallery, University of Texas,
      Austin. Traveled to Art Museum of South
      Texas, Corpus Christi and Amarillo Art
      Center, Amarillo, Texas. (catalogue)
      Whitney Biennial, Whitney Museum of
      American Art, New York. (catalogue)
1984 *Holly Solomon Gallery, New York.
      Five Texans in Venice, University of
      Texas, San Antonio.
      El Arte Narrativo, Museo Rufino Tamayo,
      Mexico City. (catalogue)
      Biennial III, San Francisco Museum of
      Modern Art, San Francisco. (catalogue)

1985 *Albright-Knox Art Gallery, Buffalo.
      Traveled to Contemporary Art Museum,
      Houston and Fort Worth Art Museum,
      Fort Worth, Texas. (catalogue)
      Fresh Paint, Museum of Fine Arts,
      Houston. (catalogue)
1986 *Texas Group Show*, Texas Gallery,
      Houston.
      Directions, Hirshhorn Museum and
      Sculpture Garden, Smithsonian
      Institution, Washington, D.C. (catalogue)
1987 *Texas Group Exhibition*, James Corcoran
      Gallery, Los Angeles.
1988 *Life Stories*, Henry Art Gallery, University
      of Washington, Seattle.
      Texas Art, Menil Collection, Houston.
      *Twentieth-Century Art in the Museum
      Collection: Direction and Diversity*,
      Museum of Fine Arts, Houston.
      Holly Solomon Gallery, New York.
1989 *Yellowstone Art Center, Billings,
      Montana. (catalogue)
      *Making Their Mark: Women Artists
      Today, A Documentary Survey
      1970–1985*, Art Museum, Cincinnati.
      Traveled to New Orleans Museum of Art
      and Denver Art Museum.
      Illustrious Alumni, Art Museum,
      University of New Mexico, Albuquerque.
      (catalogue)
1990 *Paintings*, Georgia State University Art
      Gallery, Atlanta.
1991 *Melissa Miller: The Artist's Eye*, Kimball
      Art Museum, Fort Worth, Texas.
1992 *Mind and Beast: Contemporary Artists
      and the Animal Kingdom*. Traveling
      exhibition organized be Leigh Yawkey
      Woodson Art Museum, Wassau,
      Wisconsin.
1993 *43rd Biennial Exhibition of Contemporary
      American Painting*, Corcoran Gallery of
      Art, Washington, D.C. (catalogue)

Bibliography

Allison, Sue. "Her Infinite Variety." *Life:* June 1989.
Ashbery, John. "Biennials Bloom in Spring."
Newsweek: April 18, 1983.
Brenson, Michael. "Kim MacConnell and Melissa
Miller." *New York Times:* May 11, 1984.
_____. "Art: The Wild Kingdom Shown
by Melissa Miller." *New York Times:* December
15, 1985.
_____. "Why Asian Culture Answers the
Needs of Western Artists." *New York Times:*
April 20, 1986.
_____. "Landscapes of the Post-Modern
Era." *New York Times:* January 13, 1989.
Cameron, Daniel. "Biennial Cycle." *Arts:* June
1983. 64–67.
Chadwick, Susan. "Writers, Artists Present United
Front Worth Investigating." *Houston Post:*
January 24, 1988.
Gambrell, Jamey. "Texas: State of the Art." *Art in
America:* March 1987. 115–129.
Glueck, Grace. "When Artists Portray Utopia &
Armageddon." *New York Times:* January 15, 1984.
Hill, Ed and Susan Bloom. "Melissa Miller."
Artforum: January 1987.
Hoelterhoff, Manuela. "Whitney Double: No Blue
Faces." *Wall Street Journal:* April 15, 1983.
Johnson, Patricia C. "Painting Myth, Magic."
Houston Chronicle: November 9, 1990.
Larson, Kay. "All-American Energy." *New York:*
April 11, 1983.
_____. "Fresh Paint." *New York:* June
17, 1985.
Levin, Kim. "The Day Before." *Village Voice:*
January 3, 1984.
Lewis, Jo Ann. "The Texas Trend." *Washington
Post:* March 8, 1986.
O'Brien, Glenn. "Melissa Miller, Holly Solomon
Gallery." *Artforum:* October 1984.
Richard, Paul. "At the Hirshhorn, A Jarring
Experience of the Oddly Uneven." *Washington
Post:* February 8, 1986.
Rose, Barbara. "Rule Breakers." *Vogue:* June 1985.
Russell, John. "Why the Latest Whitney Biennial
is More Satisfying." *New York Times:* March 25,
1983.
_____. "American Art Gains New
Energies." *New York Times:* August 19, 1984.
Vander Lee, Jana. "Texas Art, Hot and Heavy."
Artspace: Fall 1982.

MANUEL OCAMPO

Born 1965, Quezon City, Philippines
Lives Los Angeles

Education

1984– University of the Philippines, Quezon City
1985
1986   California State College, Bakersfield

Selected Exhibitions

1985   *Bahagari 1*, Philippine International
       Convention Center, Manila.
       UNICEF Art Exhibition, Cultural Center of
       the Philippines, Manila.
       Group Show, Vargas Museum, Quezon
       City, Philippines.
1986   *Lengua Ni Utak*, Galeria de Antipolo,
       Antipolo, Rizal, Philippines.
       Group Show, City Gallery, Manila.
1987   *Salon des Independants*, Richard Benett
       Gallery, Los Angeles.
       The I Love Jesus Show, La Luz de Jesus
       Gallery, Los Angeles.
       I Just Stopped Off For A Beer, Kulay Diwa
       Gallery, Manila.
1988   *Lies, False, Hopes, and Megalomania*,
       La Luz de Jesus Gallery, Los Angeles.
       Smaller Than a Breadbox... S.I.T.E.,
       Culver City, California.
       New Art—New Artists, Francine Ellman
       Gallery, Los Angeles.
1989   *I Have No Story To Tell*, Onyx Gallery,
       Hollywood.
       The Scream Show, A.T.A. Gallery, San
       Francisco.
       Day of the Dead Show, La Luz de Jesus
       Gallery, Los Angeles.
1990   *El Filibusterismo*, Christopher John
       Gallery, Santa Monica, California.
       Substancias Irritantes, Guggenheim
       Gallery, Chapman College, Orange,
       California.
       New Work, Christopher John Gallery,
       Santa Monica, California.
       Collaborations, La Luz de Jesus Gallery,
       Los Angeles.
       Art Cafe, Municipal Art Gallery, Los
       Angeles.
       Enigmatic Messages, John Thomas
       Gallery, Santa Monica, California.
       4 Fanaticists, Action Gallery, Los
       Angeles.
       Asian American Art, L.A. Arts Festival
       1990, Korean Cultural Service, Los
       Angeles.
       Oppression—Four Voices, John Thomas
       Gallery, Santa Monica, California.

1991   *Fred Hoffman Gallery, Santa Monica,
       California.
       M.J.O., Jay Chiat Residence, New York.
       *Mike Bidlo, Manuel Ocampo, Andres
       Serrano*, Saatchi Collection, London.
       *Individual Realitities In the California Art
       Scene*, Sezon Museum of Art, Tokyo.
1992   *Matrix*, Art Museum, University of
       California, Berkeley.
       Grupo de Gago, Weingart Center
       Gallery, Occidental College, Los Angeles.
       Helter Skelter: L.A. Art in the 90s,
       Museum of Contemporary Art, Los
       Angeles. (catalogue)
       Culture Bites, California State University,
       Sonoma.
       From the Studio, Oakland Museum,
       Oakland, California.
       Documenta IX, Kassel, Germany.
       (catalogue)
       City Library, LACE, Los Angeles.
1993   *43rd Biennial Exhibition of Contemporary
       American Painting*, Corcoran Gallery of
       Art, Washington, D.C. (catalogue)

Bibliography

Baker, Kenneth. "Helter Skelter: A Defining
Moment in Los Angeles Art." *San Francisco
Chronicle:* March 19, 1992.
Curtis, Cathy. "Strong Works by Young Artists..."
Los Angeles Times: April 9, 1990.
Drohojowska, Hunter. "L.A. RAW." *ARTnews:*
April 1992.
Gardner, Colin. "Helter Skelter." *Artforum:* April
1992.
Kent, Sarah. "Fake's Progress." *Art:* London,
November 1991.
Kimmelman, Michael. "Helter Skelter Reveals the
Evil of Banality." *New York Times:* March 22, 1992.
Knight, Christopher. "An Art of Darkness." *Los
Angeles Times:* January 1, 1992.
Lawrence, Michael. "Manuel Ocampo at
Christopher John." *Art in America:* January 1991.
Liebman, Lisa. "Documenting Documenta."
Interview: June 1992.
Madoff, Steven Henry. "Documenta IX/More is a
Mess." *ARTnews:* September 1992.
Plagens, Peter. "Welcome to Manson High."
Newsweek: March 2, 1992. 65–66.
Schjeldahl, Peter. "The Documenta of the Dog."
Art in America: September 1992.
Slesin, Suzanne. "Village, Sweet Village." *New
York Times:* July 23, 1992.
Weintraub, Bernard. "Art and the Underside of
Los Angeles." *New York Times:* March 4, 1992.
Zimmer, William. "Culture Bites, Slices of Modern
Life." *New York Times:* February 23, 1992.

DEBORAH OROPALLO

Born 1954, Hackensack, New Jersey
Lives Oakland, California

Education

1975 Leo Marchutz School of Drawing and
Painting, Aix-en-Provence, France
1979 Alfred University, Alfred, New York (BFA)
1982 University of California, Berkeley (MA)
1983 University of California, Berkeley (MFA)

Fellowships and Awards

1977 Fine Art Award, Alfred University, Alfred,
New York
1982 Ann Bremer Award, University of
California, Berkeley
1987 Engelhard Award, I.C.A., Boston
1988 Art Space, San Francisco
1990 Art Space, San Francisco
1991 National Endowment for the Arts

Selected Exhibitions

1979 *Solo Show, Alfred University, Alfred,
New York.
1980 4th Western Drawing Exhibit, Albright-
Knox Museum, Buffalo, New York.
27th Annual Painting Show, Richmond
Art Center, Richmond, California.
1981 Beyond Words, San Jose Institute of
Contemporary Art, San Jose, California.
1982 Small Format Show, Richmond Art
Center, Richmond California.
1983 Current Work in California, Annual
Conference of the Museum Association
of America.
1984 59th Crocker-Kingsley Exhibition, Crocker
Art Museum, Sacramento, California.
Artists Choice, Emanuel Walter & Atholl
McBean Galleries, San Francisco.
1985 Different Directions, San Francisco Arts
Commission Gallery, San Francisco.
1986 *Stephen Wirtz Gallery, San Francisco.
1987 *Memorial Union Art Gallery, University
of California, Davis.
Passages: A Survey of California Women
Artists, 1945 to Present: Emerging
California Women Artists, Fresno Art
Museum, Fresno, California.
Oropallo/Pijoan, Raab Gallery, Berlin.
1988 *Stephen Wirtz Gallery, San Francisco.
1989 Whitney Biennial, Whitney Museum of
American Art, New York. (catalogue)
Germans van Eck Gallery, New York.
Bay Area: Fresh Views, San Jose
Museum of Art, San Jose, California.
(catalogue)

1990 *Currents, Institute of Contemporary Art,
Boston.
*Vik Muniz/Deborah Oropallo, Stephen
Wirtz Gallery, San Francisco.
*1990 Painting Award Exhibition,
Artspace, San Francisco.
Word As Image. Traveling exhibition or-
ganized by the Milwaukee Art Museum.
(catalogue)
Words As Symbols, Aldrich Museum of
Contemporary Art, Ridgefield,
Connecticut.
1991 *Greenville County Museum of Art,
Greenville, South Carolina.
*Germans van Eck Gallery, New York.
Her Story, Oakland Museum, Oakland,
California.
Cruciformed, Cleveland Center for
Contemporary Art.
1992 *Weatherspoon Gallery, University of
North Carolina, Greensboro.
*Raab Gallery, London.
Why Painting—Part I, Susan Cummins
Gallery, Mill Valley, California.
Painted Word/Written Image, Greg
Kucera Gallery, Seattle.
Somewhere Between Image and Text,
Krakow Gallery, Boston.
1993 *Stephen Wirtz Gallery, San Francisco.
43rd Biennial Exhibition of Contemporary
American Painting, Corcoran Gallery of
Art, Washington, D.C. (catalogue)

Bibliography

Baker, Kenneth. "Whitney Biennial Exhibition Is a
Clever and Cynical Mix." San Francisco Chronicle:
May 13, 1989.
_____. "3 Award Winners in Artspace
Exhibition." San Francisco Chronicle: June 30, 1990.
Berkson, Bill. "Deborah Oropallo at Stephen Wirtz
Gallery." Artforum: September 1988.
Flam, Jack. "The View From the Cutting Edge."
Wall Street Journal: May 10, 1989.
French, Christopher. "Three Different Voices."
Artweek: September 7, 1985.
Hjalmerson, Brigitta. "Sliding, Rocking & Rolling
in California." Art & Auction: November 1986.
Larson, Kay. "The Children's Hour." New York:
May 8, 1989.
Levy, Mark. "California Contemporary Art." Art &
Antiques: September 1988.
Morch, Al. "Arts Commission Shows the Work of
Promising Young Artists." San Francisco
Examiner: February 25, 1985.
_____. "Maturity Brings Out Outstanding
Talent in Two Young Artists." San Francisco
Examiner: October 14, 1986.
Porges, Maria. "Quick Quick Pause." Artforum:
May 1991. 108–112.
Smith, Roberta. "More Women and Unknowns in
Whitney Biennial." New York Times: April 28, 1989.
Tarshis, Jerome. "Deborah Oropallo at Stephen
Wirtz." Art in America: February 1987.
Temin, Christine. "ICA's Currents Takes a Look at
What's New." Boston Globe: January 23, 1990.
Thompson, Walter. "Deborah Oropallo at
Germans van Eck." Art in America: December 1991.
Turner, Elisa. "Deborah Oropallo." ARTnews:
Summer 1992.

ELENA SISTO

Born 1952, Boston
Lives New York City

Education

1975	Brown University and Rhode Island School of Design (BA)
1975–1977	New York Studio School

Fellowships and Awards

1983	National Endowment for the Arts
1987	Millay Colony for the Arts
1989	National Endowment for the Arts

Selected Exhibitions

1981   Rotunda Gallery, Brooklyn, New York.

1982   Leonarda di Maura Gallery, New York.

1983   *Art on Paper, 1983*, Weatherspoon Art Gallery, University of North Carolina, Greensboro.

1984   *Vanderwoude Tananbaum Gallery, New York.
Art on Paper, 1984, Weatherspoon Art Gallery, University of North Carolina, Greensboro.
Women Artists of the 80s: New Talent, A.I.R. Gallery, New York.
Situations, Jamaica Arts Center, Queens, New York.

1985   *Alumni Show*, New York Studio School, New York.
Notions of Surrealism, Vanderwoude Tananbaum Gallery, New York.
Twentieth Anniversary Show, New York Studio School, New York.

1986   *Vanderwoude Tananbaum Gallery, New York.
Skowhegan 40th Anniversary Exhibition, Leo Castelli, New York.
Inner Images, Colby College Museum of Art, Waterville, Maine.
Recent American Painting and Sculpture: 1975–1985, Newark Museum, Newark, New Jersey.

1987   *To Objectify the Subjective: Contemporary Symbolist Sensibilities*, Winston Gallery, Washington, D.C.

1988   Bali Miller Gallery, New York.
NYC at NV, New Visions Gallery, Ithaca, New York.
Nature in Art—44 Woman Artists, One Penn Plaza, New York.

1989   *Drawings*, Fawbush Gallery, New York.
Personal Icons, City Gallery, Department of Cultural Affairs, New York City.
Field and Frame: Meyer Shapiro's Semiotics of Painting, New York Studio School, New York.
Imminent Space, Ruggiero Henis Gallery, New York.

1990   *Damon Brandt Gallery, New York.
Fluid Geometry, Cummings Arts Center, Connecticut College, New London, Connecticut.
Eros/Thanatos—Death and Desire, Tom Cugliani Gallery, New York.

1991   *University of Missouri, St. Louis.
Peter McClennan and Elena Sisto, Germans van Eck Gallery, New York.
Personal Mythologies, Marc Richards Gallery, Los Angeles.
Examples: Cool and Lonely, Roy Boyd Gallery, Los Angeles.

1992   *Germans van Eck Gallery, New York.
Miriam and Ira D. Wallach Art Gallery, Columbia University, New York.
On Condition: Painting Between Abstraction and Representation, University of Illinois at Chicago, College of Architecture, Art and Urban Planning.
Re-Framing Cartoons, Wexner Center for the Visual Arts, Ohio State University, Columbus.

1993   *Stephen Wirtz Gallery, San Francisco.
Formative Past: Present Form, New York Studio School, New York.
Randolph-Macon Woman's College, Lynchburg, Virginia.
The Eidetic Image: Contemporary Works on Paper. Traveling exhibition organized by the Newport Harbor Art Museum, Newport Beach, California.
43rd Biennial Exhibition of Contemporary American Painting, Corcoran Gallery of Art, Washington, D.C. (catalogue)

Bibliography

Bass, Ruth. *ARTnews:* February 1993.

Brenson, Michael. *New York Times:* May 24, 1985.

Curtis, Cathy. "Sheer Madness." *Los Angeles Times:* January 15, 1991.

Hagen, Charles. *New York Times:* December 4, 1992.

_____. *Artforum:* Summer 1990.

Johnson, Kenneth. *Art in America:* June 1990.

Klein, Ellen. *Arts:* September 1984.

Mahoney, Robert. *Arts:* Summer 1990.

Raynor, Vivien. *New York Times:* June 2, 1985.

Smith, Roberta. "Peter McClennan and Elena Sisto." *New York Times:* November 7, 1986.

Westfall, Stephan. *Art in America:* February 1987.

NANCY SPERO

Born 1926, Cleveland, Ohio
Lives New York City

Education

1949   School of the Art Institute of Chicago
        (BFA)
1950   Atelier Andre L'Hote, Paris
1950   École des Beaux-Arts, Paris

Fellowships and Awards

1976   New York State Council on the Arts
1977   National Endowment for the Arts
1991   Honorary Doctorate, School of the Art
        Institute of Chicago

Selected Exhibitions

1986   *Rhona Hoffman Gallery, Chicago
        *Josh Baer, New York
        *Nancy Spero/Leon Golub, Greenville
        County Museum of Art, Greenville,
        South Carolina.
        Biennial, Sydney, Australia. (catalogue)
        Image War, Artist's Call Against US
        Intervention in Central America, Center
        for Idea Art, Denver.
1987   *Nancy Spero, Works Since 1950.
        Traveling exhibition organized by the
        Everson Museum of Art, Syracuse,
        New York. (catalogue)
        *Nancy Spero, Institute of Contemporary
        Art, London. Traveled to Fruit Market
        Gallery, Edinburgh and Orchard Gallery,
        Derry, Northern Ireland.
        *Sheela and the Dildo Dancer, Josh Baer
        Gallery, New York.
        *Some Like It Hot, Washington Project
        for the Arts, Washington, D.C.
1988   *The First Language, Museum of
        Contemporary Art, Los Angeles.
        *Barbara Gross Galerie, Munich.
        *War Series 1966–1969, Artaud
        Paintings: 1969–1970, Rhona Hoffman
        Gallery, Chicago.
        *The Artaud Series: 1969–1970, Barbara
        Gladstone Gallery, New York.
        *War Paintings: 1966–1970, Josh Baer
        Gallery, New York.
        *Nancy Spero/Barbara Chavous,
        University Art Gallery, Ohio State
        University.
        Committed to Print, Museum of Modern
        Art, New York. (catalogue)

1989   *Burnett Miller Gallery, Los Angeles.
        *Contemporary Art Gallery, Vancouver,
        British Columbia.
        *Les Magiciens de la Terre, Le Grande
        Halle de la Villette, Paris. (catalogue)
        *Nancy Spero, Works from 1956–62,
        Josh Baer Gallery, New York.
1990   *Galerie Montenay, Paris.
        *Notes In Time, Honolulu Academy of
        Arts, Honolulu, Hawaii.
        *Anthony Reynolds Gallery, London.
        *Nancy Spero: Bilder 1958 bis 1990,
        Haus am Wlasee, Berlin. Traveled to
        Bonner Kunstverein, Bonn and
        Gemeentemuseum, The Netherlands.
        *To Soar II and Ballad of Marie Sanders,
        The Jew's Whore (Brecht), Smith College
        Museum of Art, Northampton,
        Massachusetts.
1991   *Jürgen Becker Galerie, Hamburg.
        *Sky Goddess/Egyptian Acrobat and
        Cabaret, Josh Baer Gallery, New York.
        *Nancy Spero in der Glyptothek, Arbeiten
        auf Paier, Glyptothek am Königsplatz,
        Munich.
        *Barbara Gross Galerie, Munich.
        *Works on Paper 1981–1991, Salzburger
        Kunstverein, Künstlerhaus Salzburg,
        Austria.
        *Nancy Spero & Leon Golub: A
        Commitment to the Human Spirit,
        University of Wisconsin, Milwaukee.
        *Vulture Goddess and Chorus Line, ICA,
        University of Pennsylvania, Philadelphia.
        Traveled to the Newport Harbor Art
        Museum, Newport Beach, California.
        *El Sueño Imperitívo, Circulo de Bellas
        Artes, Madrid.
1992   *Allegories of Modernism: Contemporary
        Drawing, Museum of Modern Art, New
        York.
        *Ulmer Museum, Ulm, Germany.
1993   *Greenville County Museum of Art,
        Greenville, South Carolina. (catalogue)
        Whitney Biennial, Whitney Museum of
        American Art, New York. (catalogue)
        Leon Golub/Nancy Spero, Josh Baer
        Gallery, New York.
        43rd Biennial Exhibition of Contemporary
        American Painting, Corcoran Gallery of
        Art, Washington, D.C. (catalogue)

Bibliography

Brenson, Michael. "Nancy Spero." New York
Times: March 28, 1986.
Dobie, Elizabeth Ann. "Interweaving Feminist
Frameworks." Journal of Aesthetics and Art
Criticism: Fall 1990. 381–394.
Hess, Elizabeth. "Collateral Damage." Village
Voice: March 12, 1991.
Holert, Tom. "Kunst Weiblichkeit im Widerstand."
Vogue: April 1992. 116–118.
Levin, Kim. "Mastery Exposed." Village Voice:
June 6, 1989.
Lubell, Ellen. "Spectacolor Short-Circuits." Village
Voice: February 10, 1987.
McEvilley, Thomas. "Nancy Spero, Josh Baer
Gallery." Artforum: Summer 1986. 123–124.
_____. "Nancy Spero: Everson Museum
of Art." Artforum: May 1988. 152–153.
Raven, Arlene. "Not a Pretty Picture: Can Violent
Art Heal?" Village Voice: June 17, 1986.
Shottenkirk, Dena. "Nancy Spero: Josh Baer
Gallery." Artforum: May 1991.
Smith, Roberta. "Collages That Seek To Fuse
Beauty and Feminism." New York Times: May 26,
1989.
_____. "Greene Street." New York Times:
February 26, 1988.
_____. "Nancy Spero." New York Times:
March 8, 1991.
Spero, Nancy. "Sky Goddess—Egyptian Acrobat."
Artforum: March 1988.

C H E C K L I S T

IDA APPLEBROOG

Empty Orchestra, 1993
Dimensions variable
Courtesy of Ronald Feldman
Fine Arts, New York

KEN APTEKAR

And How Did That Make You Feel, 1992
Oil on wood, sandblasted glass, bolts
Triptych, 30 x 90 (76.2 x 228.6 cm)
Klinger-Gal Collection

Heavy Equipment, 1992
Oil on wood, sandblasted glass, bolts
Diptych, 30 x 60 (76.2 x 152.4 cm)
Klinger-Gal Collection

Pink Frick, 1993
Oil on wood, sandblasted glass, bolts
60 x 60 (152.4 x 152.4 cm)
Klinger-Gal Collection

DOTTY ATTIE

After Courbet, 1993
Oil on canvas
63 panels, 6 x 6 each
(15.2 x 15.2 cm); 44 x 56
(111.8 x 142.4 cm) overall
Courtesy of the artist and
P.P.O.W., New York

Mixed Messages, 1993
Oil on canvas
36 panels, 6 x 6 each
(15.2 x 15.2 cm); 34 x 55
(86.4 x 139.7 cm) overall
Courtesy of the artist and
P.P.O.W., New York

Mixed Metaphors, 1993
Oil on canvas
36 panels, 6 x 6 each
(15.2 x 15.2 cm); 34 x 55
(86.4 x 139.7 cm) overall
Courtesy of the artist and
P.P.O.W., New York

LUIS CRUZ AZACETA

Po' Boys, 1992
Acrylic on canvas
72 x 36½ (182.9 x 92.7 cm)
Courtesy of Frumkin/Adams Gallery,
New York

Split Rafter, 1993
Acrylic on canvas
120 x 120 (304.8 x 304.8 cm)
Courtesy of Frumkin/Adams Gallery,
New York

Tchoupitoulas Shoot Out, 1992
Acrylic and Polaroids on canvas
120 x 120 (304.8 x 304.8 cm)
Courtesy of Frumkin/Adams Gallery,
New York

DONALD BAECHLER

Finger #1–10, 1992
Gesso, gouache, coffee and
collage on paper
17 x 14 (43.2 x 35.6 cm) each
Collection of the artist;
courtesy of Paul Kasmin Gallery,
New York

Palm, 1992
Gesso, gouache, coffee and
collage on paper
53 x 40½ (134.6 x 102.9 cm)
Collection Alan Wanzenberg;
courtesy of Sperone Westwater
Gallery, New York

Palm, 1992
Gesso, gouache, collage and
coffee on paper
53 x 40½ (134.6 x 102.9 cm)
Collection of the artist;
courtesy of Paul Kasmin Gallery,
New York

Profile with Four Palms #1, 1992
Gesso, gouache, collage and
coffee on paper
53 x 40½ (134.6 x 102.9 cm)
Collection of the artist;
courtesy of Paul Kasmin Gallery,
New York

Profile with Four Palms #2, 1992
Gesso, gouache, collage and
coffee on paper
53 x 40½ (134.6 x 102.9 cm)
Collection of the artist;
courtesy of Paul Kasmin Gallery,
New York

Three Hands (Red Version), 1992
Gesso, gouache, collage and
coffee on paper
53 x 40½ (134.6 x 102.9 cm)
Courtesy of Sperone Westwater Gallery,
New York

Three Palms, 1992
Gesso, gouache, collage and
coffee on paper
53 x 40½ (134.6 x 102.9 cm)
Courtesy of Sperone Westwater Gallery,
New York

DREW BEATTIE & DANIEL DAVIDSON

Call Me Fantastic, 1992
Oil on canvas
96 x 74 (243.8 x 187.96 cm)
Courtesy of Gallery Paule Anglim,
San Francisco

School of Dogs, 1992
Oil on canvas
96 x 84 (243.8 x 213.4 cm)
Courtesy of Gallery Paule Anglim,
San Francisco

**The Midnight Ride of
Paul Revere**, 1993
Oil on canvas
96 x 84 (243.8 x 213.4 cm)
Courtesy of Gallery Paule Anglim,
San Francisco

PHYLLIS BRAMSON

Apple Picker, 1992–93
Mixed media and oil on canvas
48 x 72 (121.9 x 182.9 cm)
Courtesy of Brody's Gallery,
Washington, D.C. and
Phyllis Kind Gallery,
Chicago and New York

Broken Cup, 1991–92
Mixed media and oil on canvas
48 x 72 (121.9 x 182.9 cm)
Courtesy of Brody's Gallery,
Washington, D.C. and
Phyllis Kind Gallery,
Chicago and New York

Hand to Head, 1993
Mixed media and oil on canvas
64 x 89 (162.6 x 226.1 cm)
Courtesy of Brody's Gallery,
Washington, D.C. and
Phyllis Kind Gallery,
Chicago and New York

Suddenly Its Winter, 1992
Mixed media and oil on canvas
68 x 68 (172.7 x 172.7 cm)
Courtesy of Brody's Gallery,
Washington, D.C. and
Phyllis Kind Gallery,
Chicago and New York

MICHAEL BYRON

**People Sit and Wait (Birth of
Performance Art)**, 1993
Oil and collage on canvas
27½ x 39⅜ (69.8 x 99.9 cm)
Courtesy of Galerie Philippe Gravier,
Paris

**People Sit and Watch (Birth of
Performance Art)**, 1993
Oil and collage on canvas
27½ x 35½ (69.8 x 90 cm)
Private Collection; courtesy of
Galerie Philippe Gravier,
Paris

**People Sit and Worry (Birth of
Performance Art)**, 1993
Oil and collage on canvas
27½ x 31½ (69.8 x 80 cm)
Private Collection; courtesy of
Galerie Philippe Gravier,
Paris

When Circumstances Conspire,
1991–92
Oil on panel
117¾ x 60¼ (200 x 153 cm)
Collection of the artist

CAROLE CAROOMPAS

**Before and After Frankenstein:
The Woman Who Knew Too Much:
Bedside Vigil**, 1992
Acrylic on canvas
96 x 108 (243.8 x 274.3 cm)
Courtesy of Sue Spaid Fine Art,
Los Angeles

**Before and After Frankenstein:
The Woman Who Knew Too Much:
Observing the Natural Decay
and Corruption**, 1992
Acrylic on canvas
96 x 60 (243.8 x 152.4 cm)
Courtesy of P.P.O.W.,
New York

**Before and After Frankenstein:
The Woman Who Knew Too Much:
Spectre and Emanation**, 1993
Acrylic on canvas
60 x 48 (152.4 x 73.9 cm)
Courtesy of Sue Spaid Fine Art,
Los Angeles

ROBERT COLESCOTT

Between Two Worlds, 1992
Acrylic on canvas
84 x 72 (213.4 x 182.9 cm)
Courtesy of Phyllis Kind Gallery,
New York and Chicago

**The Atom Bomb in L.A.
(Do the Hula-Hula)**, 1992
Acrylic on canvas
84 x 72 (213 .4 x 182.9 cm)
Courtesy of Phyllis Kind Gallery,
New York and Chicago

Triumph of Christianity, 1993
Acrylic on canvas
90 x 114 (228.6 x 289.6 cm)
Courtesy of Phyllis Kind Gallery,
New York and Chicago

KIM DINGLE

Black Girl Dragging White Girl, 1992
Oil and charcoal on linen
72 x 60 (182.9 x 152.4 cm)
Collection Corcoran Gallery of Art,
Gift of the Women's Committee

Girl Boxing, 1992
Oil on linen
72 x 60 (182.9 x 152.4 cm)
Collection Susan and Michael Hort

**To All the Girls of
Foreign Wars**, 1992
Oil on canvas
72 x 96 (182.9 x 152.4 cm)
Collection Jeffery A. Dash

**White Girl Trying to
Lift Black Girl**, 1992
Oil on linen
72 x 60 (182.9 x 152.4 cm)
Collection ARA Services

INGA FRICK

**Black and White and
Read All Over**, 1992
Acrylic on fabric
Triptych, 76¾ x 211¼
(194.9 x 536.6 cm)
Courtesy of Jones Troyer
Fitzpatrick Gallery,
Washington, D.C.

Chatterbox, 1992
Acrylic on fabric
76¾ x 96 (194.9 x 243.8 cm)
Courtesy of Jones Troyer
Fitzpatrick Gallery,
Washington, D.C.

Shadow Box, 1992
Acrylic and pencil on fabric
76¾ x 96 (194.9 x 243.8 cm)
Courtesy of Jones Troyer
Fitzpatrick Gallery,
Washington, D.C.

CHARLES GARABEDIAN

Study for the Iliad, 1992
Acrylic and paper on panel
43¼ x 80¼ (109.9 x 203.8 cm)
Courtesy of the artist,
L.A. Louver, Inc., Venice, California,
and Gallery Paule Anglim,
San Francisco

Study for the Iliad, 1992
Acrylic on panel
48 x 60 (121.9 x 152.4 cm)
Courtesy of the artist,
L.A. Louver, Inc., Venice, California,
and Gallery Paule Anglim,
San Francisco

Study for the Iliad, 1992
Acrylic on paper
43½ x 104 (109.9 x 264.2 cm)
Courtesy of Gallery Paule Anglim,
San Francisco

Study for the Iliad, 1992
Acrylic on panel
48 x 36 (121.9 x 91.4 cm)
Courtesy of the artist,
L.A. Louver, Inc., Venice, California,
and Gallery Paule Anglim,
San Francisco

Study for the Iliad, 1992
Acrylic on paper
33 x 43 (83.8 x 109.2 cm)
Courtesy of the artist and L.A. Louver, Inc.,
Venice, California

LEON GOLUB

Agent Orange, 1993
Acrylic on linen
56 x 88 (142.2 x 223.5 cm)
Courtesy of the artist and
Josh Baer Gallery, New York

Jubilance, 1993
Acrylic on linen
76 x 121 (193 x 307.3 cm)
Courtesy of the artist and
Josh Baer Gallery, New York

Lady Love, 1993
Acrylic on linen
28 x 68 (71.1 x 172.7 cm)
Courtesy of the artist and
Josh Baer Gallery, New York

So Much the Worse, 1993
Acrylic on linen
68½ x 131 (174 x 332.7 cm)
Courtesy of the artist and
Josh Baer Gallery, New York

Trust Me, 1993
Acrylic on linen
48 x 46 (121.9 x 116.8 cm)
Courtesy of the artist and
Josh Baer Gallery, New York

CATHERINE HOWE

Frozen Sounds, 1992
Oil on canvas
52 x 40 (132.1 x 102.6 cm)
Collection Tom Patchett,
Los Angeles

Mirage, 1993
Oil on linen
84 x 60 (213.4 x 152.4 cm)
Collection Alan P. Power,
Venice, California

Pink Arabesque, 1992
Oil on linen
84 x 60 (213.4 x 152.4 cm)
Collection of Claudio and Paola Bordignon

The Web, 1992
Oil on canvas
82 x 58 (208.3 x 147.3 cm)
Rubell Family Collections,
New York

DAVID HUMPHREY

First Supper, 1992
Oil on canvas
72 x 82 (182.9 x 208.3 cm)
Courtesy of McKee Gallery,
New York

Guest, 1993
Oil on canvas
72 x 56 (182.9 x 142.24 cm)
Courtesy of McKee Gallery,
New York

Your Sponge, 1992
Oil on canvas
82 x 72 (208.3 x 182.9 cm)
Courtesy of McKee Gallery,
New York

HUNG LIU

Mona Lisa II, 1992
Oil on canvas, with
lacquered wood and antique
architectural fragments
42 x 30 (106.7 x 76.2 cm)
Collection Frances Scher;
Courtesy Steinbaum Krauss Gallery,
New York

Raft of the Medusa, 1992
Oil on canvas with lacquered wood
and mixed media
61 x 96 x 8½
(154.9 x 243.8 x 21.6 cm)
Collection Eric and Barbara Dobkin

Swan Song, 1993
Oil on canvas and
mixed media
61 x 91⅝ x 3
(154.9 x 232.7 x 7.6 cm)
Courtesy of Rena Bransten
Gallery, San Francisco

JIM LUTES

Tire Party, 1992
Acrylic on linen
57 x 69 (144.8 x 175.3 cm)
Collection Edie and
James Cloonan, Chicago

Too Lips, 1992
Oil on linen
60 x 42 (152.4 x 106.7 cm)
Collection Arthur G. Rosen,
New York

Pacified Night, 1993
Oil on linen
60 x 84 (152.4 x 213.4 cm)
Courtesy of Edward Thorp
Gallery, New York

KERRY JAMES MARSHALL

Could This Be Love, 1992
Acrylic and collage on canvas
85 x 92 (215.9 x 233.7 cm)
The Bailey Collection, Toronto;
courtesy of Jack Shainman
Gallery, New York

Beauty Examined, 1993
Acrylic on canvas
84 x 98 (213.4 x 248.9 cm)
Courtesy of Charles Sims and
Koplin Gallery, Los Angeles

The Lost Boys, 1993
Acrylic on canvas
104 x 120 (264.2 x 304.8 cm)
Courtesy of the Principal Financial Group
and Koplin Gallery, Los Angeles

The Lost Boys,
AKA Baby Brother, 1993
Acrylic on paper
26½ x 25½ (67.3 x 64 cm)
Courtesy of Koplin Gallery,
Los Angeles

The Lost Boys,
AKA Li'l Bit, 1993
Acrylic on paper
26½ x 26½ (67.3 x 67.3 cm)
Courtesy of Madeline Murphy Rabb,
Los Angeles

MELISSA MILLER

Decision, 1991–92
Oil on linen
51 x 76 (129.5 x 193 cm)
The Barrett Collection,
Dallas

Black Demon, 1992
Acrylic on paper
15⅞ x 15 (40.3 x 38.1 cm)
Courtesy of Texas Gallery,
Houston

December Heart, 1992
Oil on linen
20 x 18 (50.8 x 45.7 cm)
Collection Mr. and Mrs. Robert Sager

The Temptation of Saint Anthony, 1993
Oil on linen
51 x 76 (129.5 x 193 cm)
The Barrett Collection,
Dallas

Tree Angel, 1992
Acrylic on paper
9 x 7½ (22.8 x 19.1 cm)
Collection Bob and Heather Westendarp

MANUEL OCAMPO

Duro es el Paso, 1992
Oil on linen
Diptych, 96 x 96
(243.8 x 243.8 cm)
Private Collection, Los Angeles;
Courtesy Fred Hoffman Fine Art,
Los Angeles

Once Again First in the World, 1993
Oil on linen
96 x 96 (243.8 x 243.8 cm)
Collection Jean Pigozzi, Geneva;
Courtesy Fred Hoffman Fine Art,
Los Angeles

Why I Hate Europeans, 1992
Oil on linen
106 x 106 (269.2 x 269.2 cm)
Private Collection; Courtesy
Fred Hoffman Fine Art,
Los Angeles

DEBORAH OROPALLO

Three-Man Patrol, 1993
Oil on canvas
Triptych, 76½ x 108
(194.3 x 274.3 cm)
Collection of Harry W. and Mary
Margaret Anderson,
Atherton, California

The Wolf, 1993
Oil on canvas
86 x 64 (218.4 x 162.6 cm)
Collection Anne MacDonald,
Tiburon, California

Woodsman, 1993
Oil on canvas
50 x 44 (127 x 111.8 cm)
Collection of Jay Pidto
and Lynne Baer

ELENA SISTO

Eve, 1991–92
Tempera on panel
16 x 12 (40.6 x 30.5 cm)
Courtesy of Germans Van Eck
Gallery, New York

Hotel, Motel and No Tell,
1991–92
Tempera on linen
16 x 12 (40.6 x 30.5 cm)
Courtesy of Germans Van Eck
Gallery, New York

Look For Me, 1991–92
Tempera on linen
17¼ x 27¾ (43.8 x 70.5 cm)
Courtesy of Germans Van Eck
Gallery, New York

Eeny Weeny Bit, 1992
Tempera on linen
29 x 17 (73.7 x 43.2 cm)
Courtesy of Germans Van Eck
Gallery, New York

Like the Mirror, 1992
Tempera on linen
18¼ x 28¾ (46.4 x 73 cm)
Courtesy of Germans Van Eck
Gallery, New York

Psyche/Bimbo, 1992
Tempera on linen
20 x 34 (50.8 x 86.4 cm)
Courtesy of Germans Van Eck
Gallery, New York

What Would I Do
Without You?, 1992
Tempera on linen
18¼ x 42 (46.4 x 106.7 cm)
Courtesy of Germans Van Eck
Gallery, New York

NANCY SPERO

Birth, 1990–92
Handprinting and printed
collage on paper
Two panels, 83 x 21
(210.8 x 53.3 cm) each
Courtesy of the artist and
Josh Baer Gallery, New York

Lilith, 1992
Handprinting and printed
collage on paper
46 x 19½ (116.8 x 49.5 cm)
Courtesy of the artist and
Josh Baer Gallery, New York

Sacred and Profane Love, 1993
Handprinting and printed
collage on paper
20½ x 888 (52.1 x 2,255.5 cm)
Courtesy of the artist and
Josh Baer Gallery, New York

The Cabaret II, 1993
Handprinting and printed
collage on paper
Diptych, 42 x 220 (106.7 x 558.8 cm)
Courtesy of the artist and
Josh Baer Gallery, New York

PHOTOGRAPHY CREDITS

Brian Albert (Donald Baechler)
Victor Arnold (Michael Byron)
William Bengtson (Phyllis Bramson)
Ben Blackwell (Deborah Oropallo)
Joseph Coscia Jr. (Ken Aptekar)
Tony Dyke (Robert Colescott)
M. Lee Fatherree (Drew Beattie &
Daniel Davidson)
Brian Forrest (Manuel Ocampo)
Frumkin/Adams Gallery, New York
(Luis Cruz Azaceta)
Mark Gulezian for Quick Silver Photo
(Inga Frick)
Bill Kennedy (Melissa Miller)
Jennifer Kotter (Ida Applebroog)
Erik Landsberg (Elena Sisto)
Scott Lindgren (Carole Caroompas)
Deborah Lohrke (Hung Liu)
William Nettles (Charles Garabedian)
Adam Reich (Catherine Howe and
Dotty Attie)
David Reynolds (Leon Golub and
Nancy Spero)
Sue Tallon (Kim Dingle)
Michael Tropea (Jim Lutes)
Chris Warner (Kerry James Marshall)
Ed Watkins (David Humphrey)

This catalogue was designed by Cynthia
Hotvedt, Washington, D.C., and typeset in
Universe Bold and Light Condensed by
Artech Graphics II, Inc., Baltimore,
Maryland. 2,000 copies were printed on
100-lb. LOE dull by Garamond/Pridemark
Press, Baltimore, Maryland.